A DESIGNER'S RESEARCH MANUAL

SUCCEED IN DESIGN
BY KNOWING YOUR CLIENTS AND WHAT THEY REALLY NEED

Jenn + Ken Visocky O'Grady

First published in the United States of America by
Rockport Publishers, a member of
Quarto Publishing Group USA Inc
100 Cummings Center
Suite 406-L
Beverly, Massachusetts 01915-6101
Telephone: 978.282.9590
Fax: 978.283.2742
www.rockpub.com

Library of Congress Cataloging-in-Publication Data

Visocky O'Grady, Jennifer.
    A designer's research manual : succeed in design by knowing your client and what they really need / Jennifer Visocky O'Grady and Kenneth Visocky O'Grady.
        p.   cm. — (Design field guides)
    Includes bibliographical references and index.
    ISBN 1-59253-257-8 (hardcover)
    1. Commercial art—United states—Marketing. 2. Graphic arts—United States—Marketing. I. Visocky O'Grady, Kenneth. II. Title. III. Series.
    NC1001.6.V57 2006
    741.6068'8—dc222006   012597
                                            CIP

ISBN-13: 978-1-59253-557-6
ISBN-10: 1-59253-557-7

Design: Enspace, Inc.
Cover Design: Enspace, Inc.

Printed in USA

This book is dedicated to designers everywhere who are pushing the boundaries of the profession to ensure its relevance, prosperity, and longevity.

PART ONE:
METHODS + THEORY

PART TWO:
RESEARCH AT WORK

CHAPTER 4:
CASE STUDIES

INTRODUCTION

If you're working for a publicly traded design megalith whose creative staff is assisted by historians, anthropologists, sociologists, and marketers, you probably don't need this book.

If, on the other hand, you're one of the thousands of graphic designers whose education was based primarily in the art department; almost all of your clients have MBAs and neutral blue swoosh logos to go with them; and you wish for some help validating your aesthetic decisions to that crowd, keep reading.

Consider this manual a primer on research methods and their practical application to graphic design. We'll broadly outline common strategies and tactics and introduce you to some creative processes in which to engage them. We'll offer suggestions for incorporating research-driven design into your creative development, whether you're a freelancer, an in-house designer, a member of a studio team, a student, or a professor. Best of all, we'll share success stories and examples of these methods in action, from designers around the globe. In every chapter you'll read an "Expert Voice," which are accessible and pragmatic accounts of real-world experiences.

Writing this book has changed the way we do business, the way we design, and the way we teach. It is our firm belief that in a profession in flux, a good generalist will always find stability. You need this information for your good generalist shelf. Know when to use it and when to call in the experts. So armed, go make good stuff.

—Jenn and Ken Visocky O'Grady

PART ONE:
METHODS + THEORY

1

AN OVERVIEW OF RESEARCH IN GRAPHIC DESIGN

WHAT IS RESEARCH-DRIVEN GRAPHIC DESIGN?

Businesses recognize now more than ever how important design is to financial success. However, clients are often looking for assurances that their communication dollars will be spent wisely. This chapter explores the concept of research-driven design, how it has been used in the past, and what tools today's designers are using to inform and ensure the success of their creative projects.

Graphic designers have long been taught that form, structure, and style are indispensable communication tools.

Hours spent in the study of typographic principles, color theory, grid placement, shape relationships, and visual contrasts inform a designer's aesthetic decisions. However, the demands placed on today's visual communication designer are very different from those asked of yesterday's commercial artist. As the design profession evolves, an increasingly competitive global marketplace expects measurable results for its creative dollars. Clients want assurance that designers understand their business issues and that commissioned work will deliver a return on their investment.

Incorporating research methods into the design process can aid in meeting this demand for a variety of reasons. Simply put, this approach redefines the designer/client relationship—and multiplies the creative and financial dividends for both. Research-driven design can help define an audience, support a concept, advocate for an aesthetic, or measure the effectiveness of a campaign. In a field dominated by subjectivity, tools such as market research, ethnographic data, Web analytics, and trend forecasting can be used to increase design commissions, communicate better with a target audience, create more effective messages, or continually assess a project's development. Applying traditional research methodology to the process of graphic design also positions the designer in a consultative role. Armed with this supporting evidence, the commercial artist (traditionally viewed

as a vendor) instead becomes a strategic consultant (newly viewed as a business partner). Though designers who base their commissions around the creation of a brochure, website, or annual report encounter clear project end-dates, those who provide strategic services often continue billing on a retainer basis.

This chapter will briefly review the historical perspectives on the role of research in design practice. Understanding how aligned fields such as architecture, interior design, industrial design, and software design have successfully embraced research can, in turn, help you learn how to apply this method to graphic design. We will also outline traditional research methodologies in order to catalogue their usefulness in visual communication efforts.

Several companies now offer inexpensive design solutions over the Internet. While quality may be an issue with many, others, such as StockLayouts.com (an Adobe Solutions Network Member) and LogoWorks.com (featured in the Wall Street Journal), benefit from valuable brand association and professional cachet.

Commodity
Example: *Envelope Manufacturer*

Specialization
Example: *Neurosurgeon*

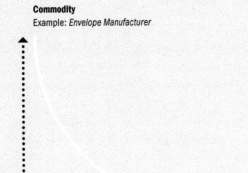

PROFIT

SKILL LEVEL + EDUCATION OF WORKFORCE

To be successful in a commodity market, industries must be capable of developing several thousand units per day, and selling them for a low price (think $25 logos, by the thousands). The other side of the scale represents individuals or organizations that have specialized skills, products, and services that the market demands at high value (think designers paid to research, consult, design, and produce artifacts at comfortable salaries). As service offerings slip down either side, more work is demanded to create products that are less valuable, making high profits harder to achieve (think the current state of the design economy, without research-driven practices).

AN HISTORICAL
PERSPECTIVE

While the concept of research-driven design may seem to be a new trend, many practitioners throughout history have incorporated research methods into their design processes.

Bauhaus Beginnings

In his book *The New Vision: Fundamentals of Bauhaus Design, Painting, Sculpture, and Architecture*, László Moholy-Nagy describes a tactile design problem assigned to second-semester students at the Bauhaus (Germany, 1919–'33) and the New Bauhaus (Chicago, 1937), where completed projects were user tested on the blind.[1] Students were asked to assemble different tactile values or "tones" in a manner that would create meaning or showcase the relationship between swatches. For example, a student might create a value scale by placing a smooth surface such as leather at one end and a rough material such as sandpaper at the other, with graduated steps in between. Projects were then user tested by the blind, and testers' comments and experiences informed further investigations.

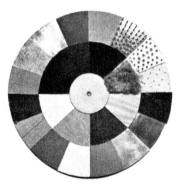

Examples

Tactile experiments may be suggested or self-imposed.
Examples:
1. A two-row tactile table, running from one extreme to the other, it being possible to touch both rows simultaneously (from hard to soft, smooth to rough, wet to dry).
2. A two-row tactile table (tactile strip) with adjacent contrasting tactile values, arranged rhythmically (Fig. 5).
3. A four-row tactile table, free arrangement (Fig. 6).
4. Free table (Fig. 7).
5. A table for vibration and pressure sensations (Figs. 8–15).

Fig. 5. Walter Kaminski (Bauhaus, second semester, 1927)
Revolving tactile table of two concentric circles with contrasting tactile values, from soft to hard, from smooth to rough.

Left, Above
In his book, The New Vision, *László Moholy-Nagy recounts the process of New Bauhaus students user-testing tactile exercises on the blind.*

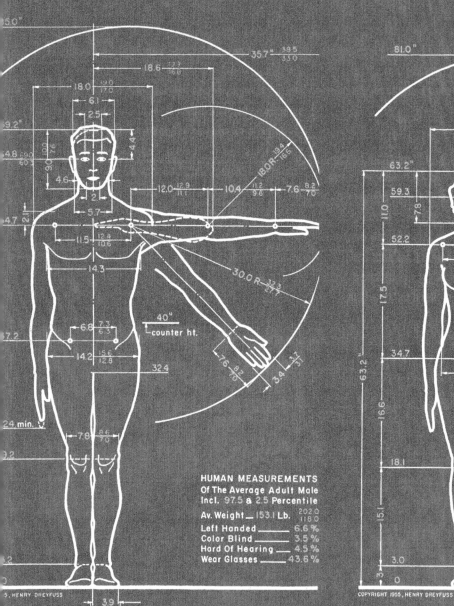

HUMAN MEASUREMENTS
Of The Average Adult Male
Incl. 97.5 & 2.5 Percentile

Av. Weight — 153.1 Lb.	202.0 / 116.0
Left Handed ————	6.6 %
Color Blind ————	3.5 %
Hard Of Hearing —	4.5 %
Wear Glasses ————	43.6 %

COPYRIGHT 1955, HENRY DREYFUSS

The Perfect Couple

Industrial designer Henry Dreyfuss dedicates an entire chapter to Joe and Josephine in his groundbreaking book *Designing for People*, first published in 1955.[2] The fictional couple originally appeared on the walls of Dreyfuss' studio as anatomical drawings of average men and women and were used to gain an understanding of human factors in product design. Dreyfuss explains that through the years Joe and Josephine developed "numerous allergies, inhibitions, and obsessions...disturbed by glaring light and by offensive coloring; they are sensitive to noise, and they shrink from a disagreeable odor." Beyond their original purpose as physical references, these insights into the feelings and needs of Joe and Josephine—user icons—gave the studio more information on which to base design decisions. This knowledge was used in the creation of everything from bicycles to tractor controls to the interiors of airplanes.

We've Been Watching You

The study of marketing research was pioneered by Arthur C. Nielsen Sr., founder of the ACNielsen company, in the late 1920s. Probably most famous for television's Nielsen ratings, Nielsen developed many innovative tools that provided clients with objective information about the effects of marketing. Using random sampling techniques, Nielsen was also able to quantify market share, making it a key indicator of financial performance. In 1939 the company expanded its operations to the U.K., with western Europe following shortly thereafter. Today they have offices across the globe, from Azerbaijan to the Ukraine, and are recognized as a world leader in marketing research.[3]

Opposite
To help guide design projects, Henry Dreyfuss personalized anatomical drawings such as these. They helped his studio to better understand the qualitative needs of end users, beyond simple anatomical factors.

Right
Most famous for television ratings, A. C. Nielsen pioneered marketing research in the 1920s.

METHODS OF RESEARCH

Though the power of design may not always be easily measured, there are many steps that practitioners can undertake to ensure that they are making informed communication choices, rather than producing artifacts rooted solely in aesthetics. Research findings can help the designer in a variety of ways. From supporting great concepts to measuring the effectiveness of finished projects, a research-driven approach can help define the way problems are solved and illustrate the value of those solutions.

BIG CONCEPTS IN RESEARCH:
A MACRO VIEW

This section provides an overview of traditional research methods and a discussion of their application to the field of graphic design. Because design artifacts (websites, brochures, annual reports, logos, etc.) are generally visual vessels for the application of research findings, it is important to begin with a survey of methods (theory), strategies (planning), and tactics (action).

QUANTITATIVE + QUALITATIVE RESEARCH

When discussing research methods, there are two distinct categories into which most data-gathering exercises fall: quantitative and qualitative.

QUANTITATIVE	QUALITATIVE
• He is 6 feet 7 inches tall	• He is tall
• They eat 6 meals a day	• They eat all the time
• The president's approval rating is at 73 precent	• The president is really well liked
• She saves $2,000 every month	• She is good with money
• The cruise ship served 3,000 passengers	• The cruise ship was huge
• The cat weighs 20 lbs	• The cat is fat

Above
Quantitative research measures objective data, whereas qualitative research measures subjective data, such as the qualities surrounding an area of inquiry.

Quantitative Research

Measuring sets of variables or quantities and their relationship to one another produces quantitative research. This form of research is built around numbers, logic, and objective data. For example, a person studying the effects of global warming may take measurements of temperature over a given amount of time to determine the rate in which the climate is changing. Though well suited to scientific pursuits, applying these metrics to creative inquiry is less successful. Instead, designers look to the social sciences for a model that better suits our specific needs. Also incorporating statistical methods, quantitative marketing research is a social research technique focused around the development of questionnaires, the responses to which can be scored and measured. In this example, if a designer wanted to determine the relationship between a Web interface and user satisfaction, the designer could ask a population of users to fill out a questionnaire. The information gathered would then be scored and measured. The resulting information could be useful in developing further iterations of the site's structure, act as a summative evaluation of the current design, or even inform future Web projects.

Qualitative Research

Whereas quantitative research deals with objective data such as numbers and logic, qualitative research deals with subjective material such as words and images. This research approach strives to understand the qualities of a specific field of inquiry. This form of investigation uses tools such as individual or group interviews, literature reviews, and participant observation to understand and explain social behavior. For example, if a researcher wanted to gain insight regarding the shopping habits of teenagers, she might spend several days on location watching the subjects at a mall or shopping center, documenting her observations. Reviewing the resulting documentation, the researcher might be able to find commonalities and thus formulate a theory on teenage purchasing behavior. In visual communication design, the majority of research practices fall under the qualitative umbrella. As designers continually develop new objects for diverse audiences, they must strive to understand the detailed needs of those consumers. Human behavior is not easily quantified; hence qualitative research strategies, born of the social sciences, are often a better fit for creative pursuits.

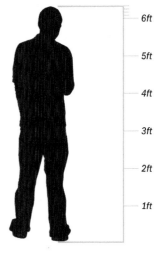

6ft

5ft

4ft

3ft

2ft

1ft

Above
An easy way to remember the difference between quantitative and qualitative research is found in the root of each word. Quantities are measurable, whereas qualities are subjective: He is 6'4" (quantitative/measurable) vs. He is tall (qualitative/subjective).

PRIMARY + SECONDARY RESEARCH

The terms *primary research* and *secondary research* might imply they happen in succession. However, they instead refer to proximity and specificity of source. Primary refers to original research that is conducted by an organization for its own use. For example, a cosmetics company in the United States might use observational research combined with surveys and questionnaires, targeted at middle school-aged girls, to determine preteen purchasing habits. They would then use the resulting data to inform their packaging, product placement, and other marketing and design elements.

Secondary research refers to the practice of reviewing a collection of data or findings that have previously been published by an outside party, for an alternative function. For example, if a record label in the United Kingdom could obtain a copy of the research produced by the cosmetics firm we've just mentioned, they might be able to use that information to aid their marketing strategies for MP3 sales to teenage girls. Chances are that reviewing the cosmetics firm's brief would be much less expensive and faster than commissioning a focus group or conducting individual interviews or surveys. The information certainly would be relevant to those planning a campaign directed at the discretionary income of an adolescent. However, lipstick and music are vastly different products. Additionally, though the subjects of both inquiries share gender and age commonality, they may well vary from a cultural perspective. Secondary investigation, though less expensive, may or may not fit the exact needs of the researcher.

PRIMARY RESEARCH	SECONDARY RESEARCH
• Commission a focus group of skateboarders, aged 12–18	• Read skateboard magazines to familiarize with youth subcultures
• Hire a marketing research firm to collect data about Aston Martin owners' mean income	• Purchase previously published demographic data about the luxury car market
• Engage octogenarians in a photo-ethnographic study at a nursing care facility	• Surf stock photography websites for images representative of seniors in nursing care facilities

Above
Primary research is conducted specifically for an individual commission. Secondary research has already been completed for a different project but may apply in some way to the current investigation.

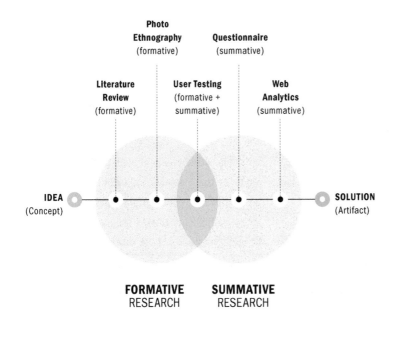

Photo Ethnography (formative)

Questionnaire (summative)

Literature Review (formative)

User Testing (formative + summative)

Web Analytics (summative)

IDEA (Concept)

SOLUTION (Artifact)

FORMATIVE RESEARCH

SUMMATIVE RESEARCH

Left
Formative research is done at the beginning of the project cycle to guide the design process. Summative research is done at the end of a project to determine its success, guage customer satisfaction, or inform future projects. Many research tactics can be either formative or summative, depending how they are utilized.

FORMATIVE + SUMMATIVE RESEARCH

Formative or exploratory research is used to gain insight into an area of study or to help define a question. This kind of research is especially useful for design applications, because in the business of innovation, identifying and then clarifying communication issues is essential. Formative research aids in problem identification and problem solving. There are a number of research tactics that could be considered formative, including (but not limited to) literature reviews, trend forecasting, video ethnography, surveys and questionnaires, demographics, and user testing.

Summative or conclusive research is used to frame and decipher the outcome of an investigative process. It confirms that the original hypothesis is correct or illustrates that it is flawed. Summative research can answer questions such as "Did I do it correctly? Did I make it better? Is it more successful?" There are many research tactics than can be summative, including

(but not limited to) focus groups, user testing, surveys and questionnaires, and Web analytics.

Most research tactics can be either formative or summative, depending where and when they are employed during the cycle of a project. For example, user testing might be performed before beginning the design of a new website, by having test subjects navigate selected URLs while tracking their responses. The data collected in those sessions would then inform navigational structures developed for the new site. A focus group could be used to determine a target audience or to evaluate a newly designed magazine cover. Observational research might be employed to assess information architecture at a library—both before new systems are implemented and afterward. The possibilities and combinations are as limitless as creativity, time, and resources will allow.

RESEARCH STRATEGIES + TACTICS:
A MICRO VIEW

Once designers embrace a macro vision of research possibilities, they are ready to access myriad strategies and tactics to further illuminate their query. Though any number of options exist, time constraints, availability, and appropriateness should be evaluated thoroughly when considering which research approach(es) to engage. In this section we will review competitor analysis, ethnographic research, marketing research, user testing, and visual exploration. These strategies employ various tactics to gather research data; throughout the course of this book we'll discuss their application to design thinking.

RESEARCH STRATEGIES	RESEARCH TACTICS
· Competitor analysis	· Literature review · Surveys + questionnaires · Focus groups
· Ethnographic research	· Photo ethnography · Visual anthropology · Observational research · Literature review · Surveys + questionnaires · Focus groups
· Marketing research	· Demographics · Focus groups · Psychographics · Surveys + questionnaires · Web analytics · Color theory + predictions · Literature review · Personas
· User testing	· Iterative design · Personas · Focus groups · Observational research · Surveys + questionnaires · Web analytics
· Visual exploration	· Visualization · Color theory + predictions

Above
For the purposes of this book, the authors have outlined several research strategies with corresponding tactics. Many of these tactics overlap into other strategic areas.

STRATEGY:
COMPETITOR ANALYSIS

Competitor analysis is the process of evaluating the strengths and weaknesses of an organization's competitors. It uses open-source intelligence—information published in the public domain (secondary sources)—to determine competitive advantages. When discussing competitor analysis, the term "competitive intelligence" frequently arises. Competitive intelligence combines the secondary source tools of competitor analysis with primary research. The goal of both strategies is the same, but competitive intelligence often employs much more aggressive tactics. Some corporations have gone as far as hiring "informants" on their competitor's staff, or releasing—and then rehiring—an employee after he or she has worked for the competition. Many businesses now use non-compete clauses and confidentiality agreements in an effort to prevent such practices. For the purposes of this discussion of research techniques and how they aid design practice, competitor analysis is a useful and ethical strategy.

There are several ways to conduct competitor analysis, the most common being competitor profiling and media scanning. Competitor profiling requires an in-depth understanding of the business or organization being evaluated. The assembled profiles may include information about the company's history, finances, products, markets, facilities, personnel, brand position, and marketing strategies. Think of competitor profiling like personas for companies (read more about personas on page 56). Media scanning—a form of open-source intelligence gathering also referred to as a literature review or communications audit—requires careful consideration of a competitor's publicly available corporate communications (such as annual reports and press releases), ad placement, messaging, and discernible brand presence. By knowing the competitor's media buying habits and brand position, the researcher can offer counter positions.

Competitor analysis is a feasible research strategy for many designers. While careful investigations may be time intensive, they can prove very beneficial when applied to a larger communication campaign. The information gathered can help determine messaging, media buys, target audiences, and other factors, and is essential to differentiating a client from other companies in their marketplace.

Surveys and questionnaires (discussed in Marketing Research, page 48) and focus groups (page 40) are other tactics frequently employed during competitor analysis.

Right
Media scanning involves scrutinizing information published in a variety of media channels in the public domain about a client's competition.

Below
This diagram depicts the numerous tactics that can be employed for competitor analysis. (In this diagram and others like it throughout the book, topics in bold will be introduced as part of the section discussion.)

TELEVISION   RADIO

INTERNET   PRINT MEDIA

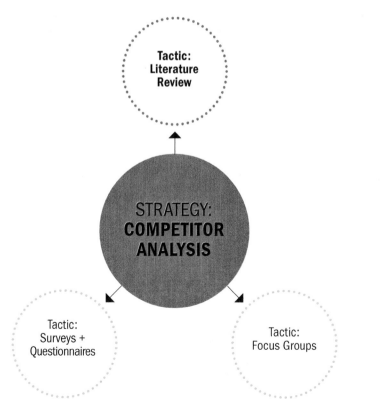

Tactic:
Literature
Review

STRATEGY:
COMPETITOR
ANALYSIS

Tactic:
Surveys +
Questionnaires

Tactic:
Focus Groups

Tactic: Literature Review

↓

What is it?

A literature review is a comprehensive investigation of all documents, publications, articles, and books regarding a specific area of study. This first step in the research process can also include a client's corporate communications, as well as those of their competitors, in which case it is often referred to as a communications audit.

What can it do?

A literature review is an important initial step, allowing the researcher to become familiar with historical references and parallel associations, as well as current market conditions. Literature reviews can also clarify research problems and be influential in the development of investigation strategies during later phases of the creative process.

How is it used?

Use literature reviews to save time. A comprehensive literature review will ensure that the researcher does not redouble efforts undertaken during previous investigations of the same subject.

When is it used?

Literature reviews are a formative tactic, used to orient the researcher to the current body of knowledge in that area. In client/designer relationships, a literature review can be undertaken to gain insight into corporate culture, competitor analysis, and market trends. It can even influence media buying practices.

Level of difficulty/complexity

Literature reviews are a relatively easy task compared to many of the other forms of investigation discussed in this chapter. Literature reviews require a strategy for finding and extracting relevant information, which can be aided by the help of a librarian. Librarians, whether at community or university institutions, are trained professionals who have extensive knowledge of and access to proprietary research tools. They can help guide a search and may also assist in locating source materials.

Note: Literature reviews are often undertaken as a starting point for other research strategies.

Opposite
Many universities and libraries house special collections that may provide valuable information and imagery unavailable anywhere else. The Cleveland Memory Project (CMP) at Cleveland State University is a good example of such a collection. The CMP special collection might become an invaluable resource for designers working for a company or civic organization headquartered in Cleveland, or for those outside the region working on a project about historic American cities or the Midwest. It could even be used as a historical reference source for display typography.

STRATEGY:
ETHNOGRAPHIC RESEARCH

Ethnography is a research strategy, created by anthropologists, that focuses on the link between human behaviors and culture. Ethnographers strive to understand and separate the emic perspective (pronounced *ee-mik*) from the etic perspective (pronounced *eh-tik*). Emic investigations define cultural phenomena through the perspective of the community under study. For example, to develop an emic understanding of graphic designers, one might conduct individual interviews directly with practicing design professionals. Etic investigations define cultural phenomena from the perspective of an individual who is not a participant in the community under study. So an etic view of graphic designers might be found by interviewing their clients or family members. Ethnographic researchers try to focus their efforts on understanding the internal, or emic, perspective of the community, using etic perspectives only to augment the data gathered by the emic study.

When choosing subjects for ethnographic study, geographic clusters, interests, ages, or a variety of other segmentation criteria can be used. Macro-ethnography studies large populations of people, whereas micro-ethnography, conversely, focuses on smaller populations. When a community has been chosen, the ethnographer—sometimes called a field worker, or field researcher—will conduct background research and identify a specific question to be examined. Immersion in the chosen culture is sometimes necessary for the ethnographer to gain acceptance (subjects won't act "naturally" if they are uncomfortable or anxious about observation). The researcher may identify key "informants," who lead them to other informants, using a snowball sampling method to conduct interviews and re-interviews over an extended period of time. These interviews use open-ended questions to draw more details from the subject. Rigorous documentation of interviews as well as copious field notes are required. After researchers have developed a theory, they may return to the group to test that assumption.

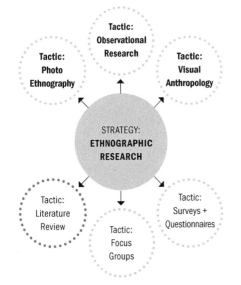

Left
This diagram depicts the numerous tactics that can be employed to collect ethnographic research.

Though Ethnography is qualitative research, the subjective observations made by the researcher are considered to be as much, if not more, valuable than any quantitative or objective data that may exist about the chosen community. This research strategy is considered subjective for several reasons:

· *Some researchers may have previous experience with the group they are studying, while others may have no prior exposure at all. Therefore, observations collected by multiple researchers may occasionally conflict. Ethnographic research experiments can never be exactly replicated.*

· *No matter how objective the researcher tries to be, it is impossible to separate personal worldview from interpretive observations.*

· *The researcher's own cultural background and personal history may skew the data.*

Ethnographers are expected to be reflexive in their work. This means that they are expected to document their own process of research as well as give insight to their own personal backgrounds, experiences, and perspectives. Including this information in a published study will enable readers to draw their own conclusions about influences that might affect the author's impartiality. Good researchers will also use several different tools to document the experiences leading up to their conclusions. This "triangulation" of interviews, recordings, field notes, and photographs helps confirm the researcher's distilled observations. Additionally, many ethnographic inquiries occur over an extended period of time, as the deep immersion of the researcher adds to the validity of the study.

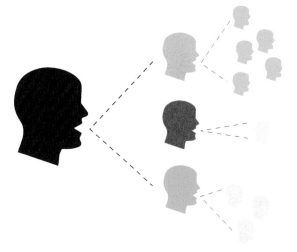

Left
Ethnographers use snowball sampling to find participants, called informants, for their studies. Informants lead to others, who then lead to more, and so on. A broad sampling is necessary to provide the researcher with an *accurate representation of the emic perspective of the group under study.*

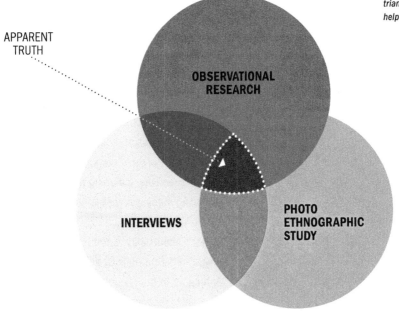

APPARENT
TRUTH

OBSERVATIONAL
RESEARCH

INTERVIEWS

PHOTO
ETHNOGRAPHIC
STUDY

Left
Ethnographers use a combination of research techniques to triangulate their research. This helps validate their findings.

Because ethnographic research involves the study of and interaction with human beings, researchers must make certain ethical considerations before engaging in fieldwork. With rare exceptions, the community under investigation must be made aware of the intentions of the study and must agree to participate. The American Anthropological Association's statement on professional ethics is a good resource for ethical guidelines.[4]

Literature reviews (discussed in Competitor Analysis, page 24), surveys and questionnaires (discussed in Marketing Research, page 48), and focus groups (discussed in Marketing Research, page 40) are other tactics frequently employed when undertaking ethnographic investigations.

Above
Macro ethnography refers to the study of large populations, such as the Japanese, where micro ethnography studies smaller populations of people, such as professional cyclists. Researchers can segment communities of study by any number of criteria.

EXPERT VOICES

Ethnography, A Research Tool for Understanding People

Ethnography is a philosophical approach to human knowledge that says it's best to understand people based on their own categories of thought, behavior, and actions. It is often used when intimate knowledge about people is needed to define a new way of thinking about a design problem and its potential solutions.

By Dori Tunstall, Ph.D,
Associate Professor of Design
Anthropology

School of Art & Design
University of Illinois at Chicago
Chicago, Illinois, USA

Ethnography is not just a series of research techniques, which may include observation, field studies, interviews, shadowing, and home tours. It is the objective of the ethnographic approach—obtaining information about people from their own perspective—that distinguishes it from other research fields such as military intelligence, which engages in observation, or journalism, which relies on interviews.

Ethnography does not happen in a laboratory. Ethnographers conduct field studies or do home tours because those places better reflect people's own values and objects. It's also easier for people to talk about their values and objects when they are surrounded by them.

Ethnography is good for answering how and why; it is not meant to answer how many. As a form of qualitative research, it is focused on providing deep understanding. When combined with quantitative approaches such as statistics, it can address the question of how many.

A trained ethnographer is someone who can make sense of all the available information to solve a design problem. Although he or she will be good at collecting information from people, a trained ethnographer is even better at helping to find the best approach and provide relevant insights for your particular solution.

Ethnography can help you discover new opportunities or better define a potential design for a specific group of people. The ability to understand people from their own perspective is a valuable skill in any work situation as well as in life.

Tactic: Photo Ethnography

What is it?

Photo ethnography is a field exercise in which subjects are asked to record their daily experiences with still or video cameras. Participants capture their own behaviors, motivations, and attitudes by documenting them with images over an extended period of time. Researchers then combine individual case studies to form a larger understanding of the community being studied. This practice is similar to visual anthropology because both use visual media for interpreting cultural human behavior. Visual anthropology differs by placing the camera in the hand of the researcher rather than in the hand of the subject.

What can it do?

Photo ethnography can help illuminate the emic, or internal, perspective of the community or individual under study ("How do the elderly view themselves?"). Analysis of the collected images can provide the researcher with insight into the lives, needs, and motivations of the subject(s) and may also help identify ways to communicate with them.

How is it used?

Photo ethnography should be a part of a larger research strategy and not a stand-alone exercise. As stated previously, ethnography is subjective and cannot be replicated, so other methods of data collection should be used to qualify the researcher's position.

When is it used?

Photo ethnography is often used as formative research, to help gain a better understanding of the intended audience's needs and behaviors. This kind of study can be used as a method in problem solving or problem identification.

Level of difficulty/complexity

Before undertaking a photo ethnographic study, the researcher must first complete investigations to identify participants (also called informants) representative of the larger community. Some time will then be spent training those participants on image-capturing skills (training time will vary depending on the skill; for example, operating a digital video camera and downloading the collected files is more complex than using a disposable camera). Photo ethnography can be relatively inexpensive and places control in the hands of the subject, essentially making them a self-ethnographer. An added benefit of this tactic is the psychological buy-in created by involving the subject directly in the investigation. Conversely, problems with observational validity may occur because the participants are actively aware of what they are supposed to be cataloguing and therefore may alter their "normal" behavior. Additional issues may arise if participants are not able to objectively select or capture images that accurately represent their larger community.

Right
To understand the unique culture at the Nance College of Business Administration at Cleveland State University for the design of a new viewbook, Enspace asked students, faculty, and administrators to document their personal experiences at the college with customized journals and disposable cameras.

EXPERIENCE
NANCE

THE NANCE COLLEGE OF
BUSINESS ADMINISTRATION HAS
THOUSANDS OF AMBASSADORS.
IN THE FOLLOWING PAGES, OUR
STUDENTS, FACULTY & ALUMNI
ATTEST TO THE EFFECTIVENESS OF
THE NANCE PROGRAM. HERE THEY
SHARE THEIR PERSPECTIVE ON THE
NANCE EXPERIENCE WITH WORDS
AND PHOTOGRAPHS.

Left, Below
Enspace designed this view book for the Nance College of Business Administration using information gathered from ethnographic kits, a literature review, and interviews conducted within the organization. Triangulating the research in this manner enabled the studio to capture the personality of the college while accurately articulating its mission in ways that connect with the target audience.

ETHNOGRAPHIC RESEARCH
Tactic: Visual Anthropology

What is it?

Visual anthropology is another field research tactic that uses visual media to aid interpretations of cultural behavior. Visual anthropology differs from photo ethnography by placing the camera in the trained hands of the researcher rather than in the untrained hands of a subject. These investigations can help to illuminate an etic, or external, perspective of the community under study ("How are the elderly viewed by others?"). Visual anthropology may also include a review of cultural representation in areas such as performance, museums and cultural institutions, art, film, and mass media. In these cases the investigation provides a secondary emic perspective, answering a question such as "How do the elderly view themselves?" by reviewing artwork created by octogenarians, or films directed by Clint Eastwood when in his 70s.

What can it do?

Visual anthropology provides a collection of discernible samples that help the researcher gain insight into the common cultural understandings of the community being studied.

How is it used?

Use visual anthropology studies as a method of documentation, augmenting other ethnographic research practices to illuminate understanding of a target group.

When is it used?

Visual anthropology, such as photo ethnography, is suited to formative research. Visual anthropology can help determine the behaviors, attitudes, and preferences of the target audience. Using visual anthropology as a tool may help the designer discover previously unknown factors. Information attained using this tactic can help define a problem or formulate a hypothesis.

Level of difficulty/complexity

This method of documentation addresses the problems inherent in photo ethnography by placing the lens in the hands of a trained researcher, through whose objective vantage point the relevance of events and symbols are catalogued. However, issues of observational validity still occur because the subject is aware of being under observation and thus may not behave in a truly candid fashion.

Opposite
Visual anthropologists can assess the etic view of a specific group by examining how that group is represented in the media. For example, a quick scan of these images would indicate that perceived concerns of the elderly are retirement, grandchildren, and healthcare.

Tactic: Observational Research

What is it?

Observational research is the systematic process of viewing and recording human behavior and cultural phenomena without questioning, communicating with, or interacting with the group being studied.

What can it do?

Simply observing people and phenomena, rather than conducting interviews, may provide a great deal of useful information. Through the resulting documentation of social behavior, researchers learn a great deal about attitudes and perspectives without influencing group behavior. This tactic allows for greater observational validity because the group under study is unaware of the researcher. The researcher is able to record and analyze what the subjects are actually doing, rather than what they say they are doing.

How is it used?

There are several keys to conducting successful observational research. The investigator must remain quiet and observant and try to understand the behaviors exhibited. It is important to remain objective, and therefore not interact with subjects. In this case, the researcher does not ask questions or solicit opinions—the focus, instead, is to watch and closely examine group behavior.

Observational research can be conducted in different ways. Researchers can go out into the field and record their observations, or they can record images mechanically with video cameras (for example, to study human traffic patterns in an airport). Of course, if images are recorded with cameras, it is important to the anonymous nature of the study that those devices be concealed. This kind of research can also be conducted in controlled laboratory settings—as is done in purchase labs, artificial environments in which research participants buy products. The use of purchase labs does however stray somewhat from tenets of traditional observational research, since participants do know that they are part of a study, which may influence their behavior.

When is it used?

Observational research can be used in a formative fashion, before a hypothesis is established. Notations from this process provide valuable insight into the behaviors of the target audience. Assumptions derived from observational research should be used as part of a multilateral process of discovery. They can also be used to support design decisions, as a form of empirical evidence.

Level of difficulty/complexity

To be reliable and fulfill project objectives, the investigator must be trained how to document his or her observations and must have a strong understanding of research goals. Observational validity may be higher in this case (compared to visual anthropology), as the researcher is not influenced by the subject's opinions. However, the investigator's personal bias still can skew the documentation.

Above + Below
*In visual anthropology
laboratories, such as this one
at Cleveland State University,
researchers use a combination of
video footage and field notes to
create documentary-style movies
that help explain human behavior.*

Another problem with this tactic is that only public behavior is visible. Individuals often behave differently in solitary or smaller group settings, and ethical considerations prevent hidden cameras from intruding into private scenarios. Observational research also rarely gives an indication of the true motivations driving the behavior being witnessed.

*Note: Observational research is also commonly practiced
during user testing.*

STRATEGY:
MARKETING RESEARCH

Market analysis and marketing research are two frequently confused terms. Market analysis is a quantitative business tool that measures the growth and composition of markets or business sectors. Market analysis considers elements such as interest rates, stock performance, price movements, and other measurable statistics that define the financial climate in which a business operates. For example, a manufacturing company might commission a market analysis to determine trends in outsourcing fabrication to foreign countries to help advise an appropriate location for its next assembly plant.

Marketing research, in contrast, is a form of sociology that focuses on the understanding of human behavior as it applies to a market-based economy. The term does not refer to a singular research method but rather a multilateral strategy used to describe a broad sampling of research practices surrounding consumer preferences. In this instance, that same manufacturing company might commission marketing research to determine the opinions of consumers regarding the need for a new version of a classic product. Would a new version be covetable? Would a new version replace the classic model, or is there enough consumer loyalty to support both?

Marketing research can be used to gather information about any number of marketing related issues, including new product launches, brand equity, consumer decision-making processes, the effectiveness of advertising, and even leveraging against competitors.

Depending on the question being asked or the issue under investigation, marketing research can be either qualitative or quantitative as well as formative or summative. Qualitative practices may include such tactics as focus groups, interviews, or other observational techniques. This approach often samples randomly from a large population, conducting surveys or distributing questionnaires that are then statistically scored. In an exploratory (formative) role, marketing research can be used to determine an area in need of investigation: Would the market support an offshoot of this brand specifically targeted at teenagers? In a conclusive (summative) role, marketing research can be used to better understand such things as the effectiveness of an advertising campaign or consumers' opinions regarding new or existing brands and products: What were teenagers' new brand perceptions, and did they prefer the original?

As with all well-designed research plans, the results yielded by marketing research are the most accurate when several different tactics are used to inform a conclusion, rather than depending on one tool to determine the results.

Color theory and predictions (discussed in Visual Research, page 62), literature reviews (discussed in Competitor Analysis, page 24), and personas (discussed in User Testing, page 56) are other tactics frequently employed when conducting marketing research.

Right
This diagram depicts the numerous tactics that can be employed to collect marketing research.

STRATEGY:
MARKETING RESEARCH

Tactic:
Psychographics

Tactic:
Focus Groups

Tactic:
Surveys + Questionnaires

Tactic:
Demographics

Tactic:
Web Analytics

Tactic:
Literature Review

Tactic:
Color Theory + Predictions

Tactic:
Personas

Personas
(formative)

Questionnaire
(summative)

Demographics
(formative)

Focus Groups
(formative + summative)

Web Analytics
(summative)

IDEA
(Concept)

SOLUTION
(Artifact)

FORMATIVE
MARKETING
RESEARCH

SUMMATIVE
MARKETING
RESEARCH

Left
Many of the tools used in marketing research are effective in the formative phases of a project when outlining a research or design strategy—or as a summary to gauge the results of a creative campaign.

Tactic: Demographics

What are they?
Demographics are collections of statistical data that describe a group of people or a market segment. Demographics generally include information on a variety of quantifiable cultural, economic, and social characteristics.

What can they do?
By grouping people into segments based on demographic variables, researchers can use the collected data to create hypothetical profiles. This research tactic can provide insight regarding what groups of people are doing, thinking, or buying. Common demographic variables include: age, gender, sexual orientation, household size, personal income and family income, education, race, and religion.

How to use them?
Researchers study demographic data to clarify their understanding of the needs and motivations of individual market segments.

When are they used?
Demographics provide formative information and therefore should be used at the start of a project to define an audience.

Level of difficulty/complexity
Marketing research firms can be hired to conduct primary demographics using proprietary resources and software. In addition, access to demographic information collected by both for-profit and nonprofit organizations is widely available as a form of secondary research. It is important to note that demographic profiling often makes broad generalizations about groups of people that do not account for the unique qualities of individuals—who may not always behave in the predicted fashion.

Right, Opposite
These charts, created from content found in U.S. Census reports, show both the macro and micro sets of data collected about the U.S. economy. Designers can use this information as secondary research.

United States Census Regions

West Mountain · West North Central · East North Central · New England · Mid Atlantic · West Pacific · West South Central · East South Central · South Atlantic

United States Economy by Industry:

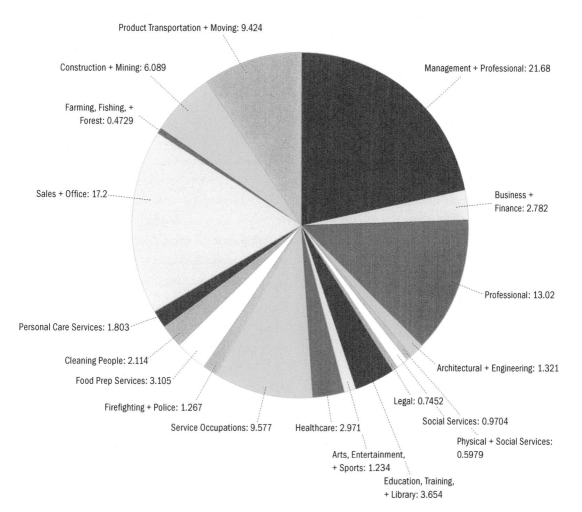

Composition of U.S. Poverty Population
Official + Experimental by age: 1992

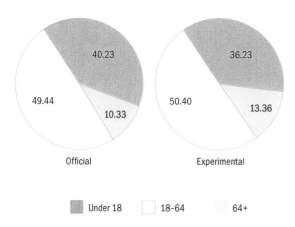

Official   Experimental

▨ Under 18   □ 18–64   ▨ 64+

Tactic: Focus Groups

What are they?

Focus groups are a social science tool used prevalently to conduct market research. Focus groups are organized discussions with a limited number of participants, led by a moderator. The goal of these discussions is to gain insight into the participants' views about a given topic. Unlike survey research, which is primarily quantitative, focus groups are qualitative exercises because they allow the researcher to understand the opinions and attitudes of the respondents. This type of research is different from the similar methods of one-on-one interviewing and group interviews, as it allows for interaction among the participants.

What can they do?

A focus group allows for interpersonal communication and interaction between participants. This kind of dialogue can lead to new topics of discussion originally unforeseen by the researcher. Additionally, participants know that their opinions are valued, or that they are considered experts—leading them to feel ownership of the process and provide possible solutions. Also, focus group research can be done relatively quickly without huge demands on time and fiscal resources. Qualitative in nature, focus groups don't require the same number of participants/responders as survey or poll research and can therefore be assembled and evaluated in a more timely fashion.

How to use them?

Moderating the session well is key to collecting viable data. It is important to make sure that participants stay focused on the questions asked, while giving them room to deviate should new issues arise. All participants must also feel that they are being engaged by the group and feel comfortable enough to participate in the discussion. Most important, the moderator must stay neutral so that he or she does not ask leading questions that might skew the data.

Focus groups usually consist of six to ten people. If the group is too small, the conversation may lag or be dominated by a few individuals. Conversely, if the group is too large, discourse may become too difficult for the moderator to facilitate. Large groups may also lead to distracting side discussions among respondents or cause some participants not to engage in the dialogue at all.

Individual background is an important consideration when selecting participants. It is essential to choose people with similar characteristics, backgrounds, or interests so that they feel comfortable talking to one another. If respondents are on the opposite ends of an issue, the conversation can become heated, preventing a free exchange of ideas. Depending on the subject, several focus groups may have to be held in order to get a representative view of the issue. People also feel more comfortable sharing their opinions with people they don't know, so limit focus groups to individuals that have no prior history with one another.

When are they used?

Focus groups can be formative or summative depending on the nature of the design problem that they are addressing. This research tactic can be used to collect new information before a project starts, or at key points during an iterative creative process to get feedback from potential users in order to refine prototypes (more on iterative design on page 54). As summative evaluation, focus groups can be used to assess the acceptance of a new campaign or gauge customer satisfaction levels.

Level of difficulty/complexity

Though focus group research has many benefits, there are a couple of potential conflicts to take into consideration. As with most group dynamics, dominant personalities may sway the opinions being expressed in a certain direction. Careful selection and good facilitation on the part of the moderator can help circumvent this issue; therefore, using trained moderators is a good investment in the success of the survey. Additionally, the results of focus groups are based entirely on the assumption that the people participating are being totally honest. Often, what people say they do is radically different from what is really happening. Preparing for these scenarios, and supplementing focus group research with other forms of information gathering, will lead to more accurate results.

Focus groups are also commonly used as components of competitor analysis, ethnographic research, and user testing.

Left
To ensure a free-flowing dialogue among participants, be sure to select people who have similar backgrounds. Radically divergent opinions can create conflict.

PLAY RANDY RHOADS' HOTTEST LICKS!

JERRY GARCIA'S CUSTOM DOUG IRWIN TIGER

Guitar Player

CMP
United Business Media

FEED YOUR OBSESSION

...MBER 2005

...N YEARS GONE
...EMEMBERING
JERRY
GARCIA

DELAY PEDAL ROUNDUP

STEVE KIMOCK MASTER CLASS

BLACK DAHLIA MURDER

LES PAUL AT 90

TOM MORELLO

MY RUIN

GANG OF FOUR

ENTER NOW! GUITAR HERO 2006

U.S. $6.50   CAN. $7.50

72

25274 01010 3

15 SONGS
CHOOSE
ONE
FREE!

EXPERT VOICES

By DJ Stout, Partner
Pentagram
Austin, Texas USA

A New Focus at *Guitar Player* Magazine

When *Guitar Player* magazine was introduced, it was one of the first guitar enthusiast publications of its kind. It set a standard for the genre and had very little competition in its category. Over the years, however, the newsstand became crowded with a host of imitators who were influenced by the standards set by the original *Guitar Player*. This increased competition gradually began to hurt the publication's overall subscriptions and newsstand sales.

We were initially brought in to redesign *Guitar Player* for two main reasons: one, to increase newsstand sales and subscriptions, and two, to give the magazine a look that was skewed toward a younger audience. The prevailing assumption at the magazine was that the competitors were gaining an advantage at the newsstand because they were younger and hipper looking and because they tended to feature newer guitar talent on their covers. The executives at *Guitar Player* fretted that they had grown complacent over the years and that the magazine was tired and perceived as the "old man" of guitar magazines.

Guitar Player had done some research on their readership and demographics prior to our involvement that they provided to us at the beginning of the redesign initiative. After reading through the material, we began to work up some initial design directions that were informed by some of the findings in the reports. It seems obvious, but it became apparent in the research that guitar players really love guitars. They recognize famous guitars and brands and they consider guitars on the same level as fine art or sculpture. They love to look at and admire beautiful and interesting instruments. It was also clear in the findings that guitar enthusiasts liked to see and read about the true masters of the craft—the guitar heroes or "old masters" of the guitar world. This second piece of information seemed to counter the perception that the *Guitar Player* staff had initially relayed to us, that the guitar enthusiast wanted to see younger players featured on the cover.

One cover concept that I favored at the beginning of our early design explorations was based on these two factors found in the research material. The existing *Guitar Player* cover had traditionally featured an accomplished guitarist holding a guitar. Our notion was to take the guitar out of the musician's hands. We felt that it was obvious to the reader that the personality featured on the cover was a guitar player considering that the magazine was actually called *Guitar Player* so there was no need to show the cover artist holding or playing a guitar every time. This freed up the constraint of always having to show the featured guitarist in a full-figure or three-quarter view in order to include his or her instrument in the composition of the cover photograph. This also allowed the photographer to move in tighter on the face of the subject to capture a more intimate portrait of the "guitar hero" that the research told us the reader wanted to see. We then took a sharp, beautifully lit photograph of the featured cover artist's actual guitar and positioned it across the entire top portion of the cover so that the instrument became an informative and changing element of the *Guitar Player* logotype every month. The addition of a caption to the image of the guitar informs the reader that it belongs to the featured cover artist positioned in the lower section of the cover right beneath the image of his

Guitar Player had planned to conduct focus groups in order to get comments on the publication...

or her instrument. We created many other cover directions, but this was the front-runner among the group from the start. Now it was time for the ultimate test.

Guitar Player had planned to conduct focus groups in order to get comments on the publication as it was and to see what kind of reactions and feedback they would get on their plans to change the publication editorially. As it turned out, our cover explorations coincided with the focus group timing, so we decided to test the covers as well. At first I was very worried about the decision to show the covers to the focus groups because of my experience with focus groups before.

Above + Below
These redesigned mastheads and covers for Guitar Player magazine were tested by Pentagram in focus groups in New York and San Francisco to measure feedback from key members of the publication's audience.

STEVE VAI'S "CROSSROADS" TRANSCRIPTION || GARY MOORE || THE VINES

ERIC CLAPTON || CUSTOM FENDER STRATOCASTER

Guitar Player

CMP

FEED YOUR OBSESSION

MAY 2004

ERIC CLAPTON CHANNELS ROBERT JOHNSON

DUANE ED
DAVID TO
THE DAWN OF BEE
NEW GEAR FROM NA
16 PRODUCT REVI
HAMER IMPROV, PEAVEY
TAKAMINE COOL
BOSS GS-10, AND N

U.S. $4.99

YOUR TOP 50 GUITARISTS REVEALED! || ZZ TOP

ZAKK WYLDE'S ORIGINAL "GRAIL" LES PAUL

|| THE DISTILLERS

Guitar Player

MP

FEED YOUR OBSESSION

ARCH 2004

AKK WYLDE'S EMO-ACOUSTIC HANGOVER MUSIC

THE LIVING END
JOHNNY A.
T-BONE WALKER
ERIC SARDINAS
BILL NELSON
5 NEW GURU LESSONS
19 GEAR REVIEWS!
MESA/BOOGIE STILETTO PREVIEW
EXCLUSIVE BLACK LABEL SOCIETY SONG

WINTER NAMM NEWS || GEORGE BENSON

|| THE HISTORY OF SHRED

JOE SATRIANI'S SIGNATURE IBANEZ JS1000

Guitar Player

CMP

APRIL 2004

FEED YOUR OBSESSION

WORLD EXCLUSIVE!
JOE SATRIANI PREVIEWS HIS NEW ALBUM

BONUS!
SATCH DETAILS HIS SIGNATURE PEAVEY JSX AMP

REVIEWED
KUSTOM WAV, DIEZEL HERBERT, AND MORE!

SATRIANI'S "BROTHER JOHN" TRANSCRIBED

The focus groups were conducted in San Francisco and in New York. A group of loyal, longtime readers and a group of twenty-year-old guitar enthusiasts were assembled and polled in each of the two cities. Two versions of the favored new cover direction were shown to the groups. One version that I really had pushed for included the image of the guitar across the top of the magazine but the masthead logo only said "Player" instead of the whole name *Guitar Player.* My hope was that the reader would see the guitar image and then the word "Player" and they would make the leap to *Guitar Player.* I loved this idea because it used the image of the guitar, which would be different every month, as a visual masthead logo. In the focus groups it became clear that this notion didn't work. The participants in the focus group thought that the name had been changed to just *Player,* which, they informed me, was the name of a porno magazine.

The focus groups did support our notion that the guitar enthusiast loves to look at guitars and to read about guitar masters. So the magazine went with the new design, which has turned out to be very innovative and successful at the newsstand— and has become the envy of the competition.

Tactic: Psychographics

What is it?

Psychographics is a quantitative tactic used to measure subjective beliefs, opinions, and interests. In other words, it is a quantitative tool for measuring qualitative information. Similar to demographic research, which gathers data on age, gender, race, and other factors, it instead counts information about opinions, religious beliefs, music tastes, personality traits, and lifestyles.

What can it do?

Psychographics can help the researcher gain valuable insight into the opinions and preferences of the groups being studied.

How is it used?

Use psychographics in a manner similar to the way you'd use demographics, keeping in mind that psychographics measure inherently subjective data. This research tactic, whether employed in a primary or secondary fashion, will help you clarify a creative approach by illuminating a target market's opinions and preferences.

When is it used?

Psychographics can be used for problem identification or problem solving. It is best used in the early phases of the design process in conjunction with demographic research, ethnographic research, and personas.

Level of difficulty/complexity

Most designers outsource primary psychographic studies to marketing research firms who specialize in the process. Often these are undertaken in conjunction with demographic investigations of the same group. Secondary psychographic data may be more readily available and thus more cost effective, but, as previously noted, will not be customized to the target market.

PSYCHOGRAPHIC RESEARCH	DEMOGRAPHIC RESEARCH
A quantitative tactic used to measure subjective information, for example:	A quantitative tactic used to measure factual information, for example:
· Opinions	· Age
· Religious beliefs	· Gender
· Musical tastes	· Sexual orientation
· Personality traits	· Household size
· Lifestyle choices	· Income

Above
Though demographic and psychographic research may seem similar, psychographic research attempts to quantify qualitative issues.

Tactic: Surveys + Questionnaires

↓

What are they?

Survey research is a tactic for collecting quantitative information by asking participants a set of questions in specific order. Questions are administered to a sample of individuals, representative of a larger population. If a researcher administers the questions, it is called a survey or structured interview. If participants answer questions on their own, either online or by filling out a piece of paper, it is called a questionnaire.

What can they do?

Surveys and questionnaires can be used to collect information about the opinions and preferences of a defined group, or to collect factual information, such as a census report. These investigations give the researcher the ability to collect large amounts of information from a wide population in a relatively short amount of time. Questions should be written and structured in ways to increase the reliability of valid findings; therefore, trained experts are the best resources for developing this content.

How are they used?

Use surveys and questionnaires to gather demographic (fact-based) or psychographic (opinion-based) data.

When are they used?

Use surveys as formative research, to gain insight into the opinions and desires of the target audience. This information can then be used to guide design decisions during project development. It can also be used as summative research, to support or confirm creative solutions, or to understand the effects of a creative campaign. For example, a group of frequent online shoppers may be asked to fill out a questionnaire regarding new features just added to the website they are using. Responses can be used to determine whether users are satisfied with or confused by the new tools.

Level of difficulty/complexity

Survey research can be a cost-effective tool for gathering information from a large population, and there are many companies and organizations that can be retained to help construct and administer questions. Because of the complex structure, writing, and scoring inherent in survey research, working with a specialist will help increase accuracy—missteps along the way can lead to invalid results. However, if there is no budget for outsourcing, tremendous amounts of information are available in the public domain to help guide the process.

Surveys and questionnaires are also commonly used as components of competitor analysis, ethnographic research, and user testing.

Opposite
OpinionLab uses survey research to measure user experiences for their clients' websites. Available on any site for a monthly fee, this tool can help designers by providing them with statistical reports of feedback from online visitors.

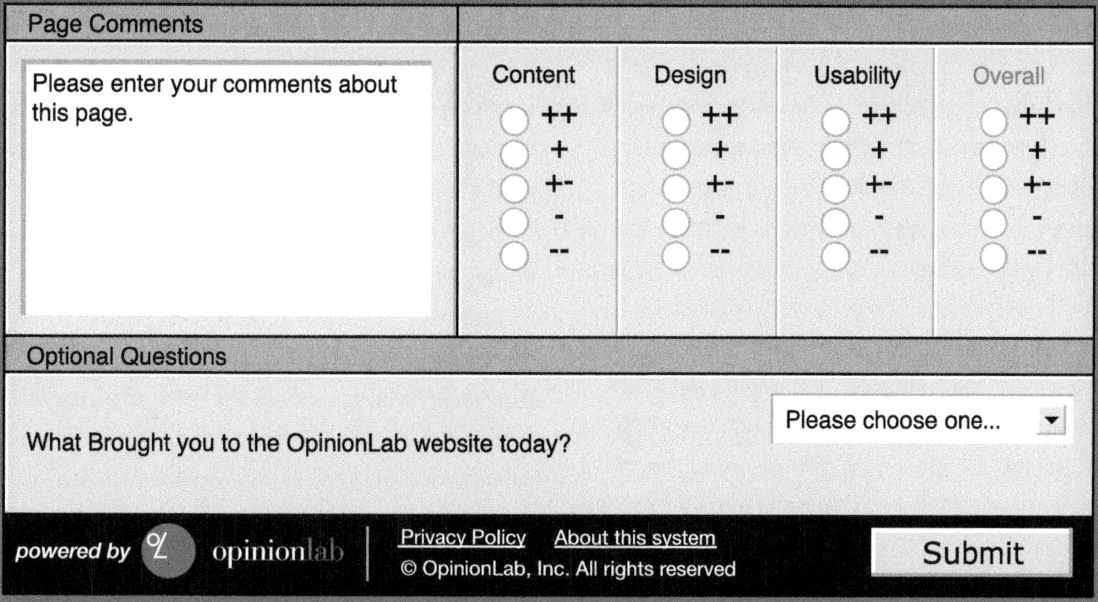

Page Comments	Content	Design	Usability	Overall
Please enter your comments about this page.	++ + +- - --	++ + +- - --	++ + +- - --	++ + +- - --

Optional Questions

What Brought you to the OpinionLab website today?

Please choose one... ▼

powered by ⊘ℒ opinionlab |

Submit

Tactic: Web Analytics

What are they?

Web analytics, sometimes referred to as Web statistics or technographic research, are a form of quantitative analysis that uses concrete metrics to track user behavior online. A designer can gain valuable insight into users' needs and interests by measuring key variables through the course of a user visit.

What can they do?

Web analytics can provide the designer with a lot of information about users' viewing habits. For example, a designer can tell where users have come from (both via geographic location and via referring Web domains); which pages are being visited most; how long users are staying on those pages; how long they stay at the site as a whole; at which times of day people are looking; and the bandwidths they are using to connect. These statistics may help the designer when thinking about where and when to run ads, based on whether the site is most commly viewed at work (high speed connection) or at home (possible dial-up modem). They can also help inform future technical considerations such as the use of video or complex interactive features.

How are they used?

Looking at technographic data for the first time can be daunting. Following are some of the basics.

Hits: A hit is a request for any file from a Web server. For example, when a user requests a Web page that has two images on it, that request will result in three hits. One hit is for the page, and one for each of the images, because all of those files are necessary to display that individual page.

Page views: Page views are a more accurate measurement of Web traffic because they indicate the use of individual pages rather than server hits. As stated in the example above, a single page view might result in several server hits because of image files, frames, style sheets, and so on.

Visits/sessions: A visit, or session, is the amount of time that a user spends on a website. For example, if a user requests a page and stays at that page for thirty seconds, that counts as a visit. When the amounts of visits are totaled for an extended period of time, the amount of traffic to the site can be determined.

Visitors/unique visitors: These terms refer to a user who visits a website more than once within a specified period of time. Web stat software is able to differentiate between visitors who come only once to the site and unique visitors who return. This information differs from a site's hits or page views—which are measured by the number of files that are requested from a site—because they are measured according to the users' IP addresses, which are unique to every computer on the Web.

When are they used?

Web analytics can produce formative and summative data. In a formative role, they can help the designer understand which features or content users find valuable in a current design. This information can then direct future iterations. In a summative role, they can tell the designer whether a redesign has increased visits, or whether a new feature is being used.

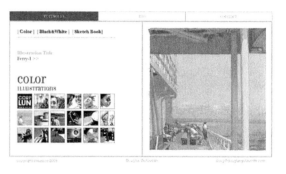

Level of difficulty/complexity

Hosting providers for websites often supply Web analytics software. Often the tools provided go far beyond these basic functions and include features that indicate the user's platform (Linux, Microsoft Windows, or Macintosh for example), bandwidth (dial-up modem or DSL?), peak usage hours, and even location. More comprehensive Web analytic studies can be outsourced to companies that specialize in evaluating this type of data. Those firms have developed proprietary tools that go beyond what a Web hosting company can provide. While this information may seem to be Web-centric, the information gathered from Web metrics can also help inform print campaigns by indicating which types of information interest users and where users are geographically clustered.

Web analytics can also be implemented in user testing.

Above

Beyond hits and visits, Web statistics can tell the designer how much time users are spending on which pages, and which pages are more popular. On illustrator Doug Goldsmith's website, for instance, statistics revealed that users on average spend a total of five minutes and sixteen seconds on their visit, with about half that time spent looking at his portfolio.

STRATEGY:
USER TESTING

User testing, also called usability testing, employs a broad range of techniques designed to measure a product's ability to satisfy the needs of the end user (accessibility, functionality, ease of use) while also meeting project requirements (budget, size, technical requirements). Usability testing is most commonly used in interactive and Web design, but many of the concepts can apply to any product intended for human use—digitally delivered or otherwise.

Usability in interactive and Web design has been linked to several key performance indicators listed below.

Staying under budget: User testing in the early stages of development, as formative research in an iterative design process (more on iterative design on page 54), will ensure that usability hurdles are cleared before the project moves to production. Correcting usability issues after a project is launched can cost significant time and money.

Higher ROI (return on investment): High usability, through user testing and iterative design, can lead to increased sales, business leads, and lower customer support costs.

Increased customer satisfaction: Sites designed with user testing practices will provide positive viewer experiences, leading to higher customer satisfaction and positive brand associations.

Many corporations and universities specialize in advanced usability testing for Web and interactive media and have labs designed around those specific purposes. User participants are asked to complete a set of "tasks": for example, locate a press release, purchase something with a shopping cart, and join a chat room. They are not given any step-by-step instructions or guidance, so the lab environment mimics a typical user experience. Participants are timed throughout the process, and often observed through double-blind mirrors. In some cases, these labs have technology that can record, in real time, the movements of a user's eyes as they navigate information on the screen. This data can be compared to the movements tracked by the user's mouse, illuminating the user's perspective on active content. Though expensive to undertake, this kind of detailed analysis is often invaluable.

Focus groups (discussed in Marketing Research, page 40), observational research (discussed in Ethnographic Research, page 34), surveys and questionnaires (discussed in Marketing Research, page 48), and Web analytics (discussed in Marketing Research, page 50) are other tactics frequently employed when user testing.

USABILITY LAB

Observation/Control Room Participant Room

Above

Usability labs are set up with the user in an observation room and researchers in a control room. The user is monitored by video cameras and researchers behind a two-way mirror while a low-voltage laser tracks the test subjects' eye movements.

Researchers can track eye movements compared to mouse movements and track how long users looked at certain pieces of information and how long it took them to perform certain tasks.

Above

Usability labs, such as this one developed by Leeds Research in Minneapolis, can help designers make decisions about design, interface, and information architecture when developing websites.

Tactic:
Personas

**Tactic:
Iterative
Design**

Tactic:
Observational
Research

STRATEGY:
**USER
TESTING**

Tactic:
Focus
Groups

Tactic:
Surveys +
Questionnaires

Tactic:
Web
Analytics

Left

This diagram depicts the numerous tactics that can be employed as a component of User Testing.

Tactic: Iterative Design

What is it?

Iterative design is based on a cycle of prototyping, testing, and refining. In iterative design, testing the project in some way—whether through focus groups, user tests, personas, or other methods—generates data to compare successive evolutions or "iterations."

What can it do?

Iterative design helps focus the final product through cycles of testing, analysis, and refinement. Questions that may have not been foreseen by other formative research may arise out of the iteration process.

How is it used?

Use iterative design to clarify communication through a series of queries (user testing) and revisions (project adjustment). Designers will benefit from an iterative process but must allow time for benchmark testing, and resulting project revisions when establishing production schedules.

When is it used?

Any number of testing/analysis/refinement cycles can be employed. These are limited only by production schedules and project budget.

Level of difficulty/complexity

The complexity of iterative design depends entirely on the tactics employed for testing and analysis. Be aware that even when using accessible techniques, the creation of multiple iterations will increase production timelines and consequentially, budgets. Because of the complexity of user needs, interactive commissions are especially good projects on which to practice iterative design.

Opposite
Using a sequence of prototyping, assessing, prototyping, and assessing, designers can use audience feedback to inform their aesthetic directions.

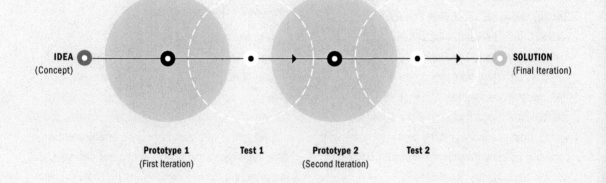

IDEA
(Concept)

Prototype 1
(First Iteration)

Test 1

Prototype 2
(Second Iteration)

Test 2

SOLUTION
(Final Iteration)

Tactic: Personas

What are they?

Personas are fabricated archetypes, or models, of end users. Personas identify user motivations, expectations, and goals. Think of a persona as a singular icon representative of an entire group. Conjecture regarding the persona's reaction in a variety of situations can help designers identify common needs.

In communication design, personas are most commonly associated with interactive work. The American firm Cooper (formerly Cooper Interaction Design) and its principal, Alan Cooper, have been pioneers in the use of this technique. In his book *The Inmates Are Running the Asylum*, Cooper explains why personas are often preferable to actual test subjects: "The most obvious approach—to find the actual user and ask him—doesn't work for a number of reasons, but the main one is that merely being the victim of a particular problem doesn't automatically bestow on one the power to see its solution."[5]

Although personas are fictitious, they represent the needs of real users and are developed through traditional research processes. This formative research is critical to being able to validate the characteristics of the model and ensure that they are not instead based on the designer's opinion.

What can they do?

Personas help guide the design process by shifting the focus directly to the user. Findings will help organize information, structure navigation, or even influence formal presentation and color choice. Because design efforts are based on these carefully researched and developed personas, the users' goals and needs are sure to be addressed. As agreed-upon identity benchmarks, personas can also help the creative team substantiate their decisions when presenting design rationale to clients.

How to use them?

Personas are created using several sources of information, including ethnographic research, focus groups, and demographic data. A brief description (maybe one to two pages long) is then created to flesh out individual attitudes, behaviors, environmental conditions, goals, personal details, and skill sets. It is important for the researcher to try to identify several different user types so that the goals of all users will be met. Keeping persona sets small ensures that the design process remains manageable, with one primary persona as a focal point.

Personas should be used as a component to a larger research strategy, not as a singular research method. Combining personas with other tools, such as user testing and marketing analysis, can give the designer valuable insight into the user's needs.

Below
By creating detailed fictitious personas, designers can develop systems that meet the needs and goals of primary and secondary users. Featured here are three abbreviated personas, created as user models for a theoretical American on-line clothing retailer.

When are they used?

Personas can be used throughout the design process. In the planning or formative phases, they can be used to align project goals with audience needs. During the creative development phase, personas can be used as a standard to measure structural or aesthetic decisions.

Level of difficulty/complexity

There is a lot of information available about the creation of personas, specifically regarding their use when designing interactive projects. However, creating functional fictitious identities takes time, so production schedules should be written accordingly.

Personas can also be used as a component of marketing research.

PERSONA #1: KENNY

- Would rather spend time riding his bike than shopping with his girlfriend

- Still buys new clothes during the "back to school" rush in the fall, even though he graduated from college 10 years ago

- Lives in the Midwest

- Works as a graphic designer and aspiring art director

- Very Web savvy, familiar with HTML and database programming and Web design principles

PERSONA #2: TERESA

- Has a dedicated "clothing" category in her monthly budget

- Shops both online and in retail stores on a biweekly basis

- Lives on the East Coast

- Works as a research analyst for a venture capital firm that funds socially relevant entrepreneurial endeavors

- Moderately Web savvy, frequently accessing the Internet at work and home via a high-speed connection

PERSONA #3: ABELINO

- Frequently entertains clients in both casual and formal social settings

- Due to time constraints, does most of his shopping online, both personal items and gifts

- Lives in Southern California but travels frequently for business

- Works in pharmaceutical sales

- Moderately Web savvy, dependent on his PDA and laptop and on hotel wireless Internet access

STRATEGY:
VISUAL EXPLORATION

Visual exploration is a method of primary research most commonly used by designers for solving problems of form and communication. Studies during this phase can include multiple variations of color, imagery, typography, and structure. Beginning with a series of thumbnail sketches and concluding with a realized prototype, this process is used to vet out the most viable graphic solution. The process of visual exploration forces creatives to move beyond initial concepts, often resulting in unique and innovative solutions.

Through the graphic testing of type and image in varying structural forms, the designer can prototype rapidly in either low- or high-tech fashion (traditional paper and pencil sketches or computer roughs). This rapid investigation allows the designer to develop grids and typographic systems that are appropriate for delivering concepts and content to the end user. This generation of multiple visual solutions allows for comparative analysis of a broad sample of possibilities, which enables the designer to see the most successful vehicle for communication. A spirit of experimentation, openness to new ideas, and rapid prototyping without fear of failure are key to this developmental process.

Visual exploration occurs after formative research has been completed. Using the information collected, the designer now focuses on creating visual prototypes engineered to meet the needs outlined during the research phase. Traditional sketching with pencil and paper remains the dominant form of rapid investigation, though designers develop their own methodology over time. Deadlines and budgets necessitate that these systematic visual development processes are executed fluidly.

Tactic: Visualization ← STRATEGY: VISUAL EXPLORATION → Tactic: Color Theory + Predictions

Above
This diagram depicts the tactics that can be employed for visual exploration.

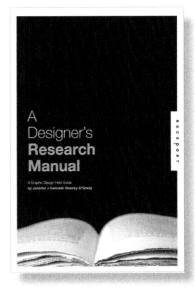

OPEN BOOK
STUDY
READING

STACK OF
BOOKS. TITLE
WRITTEN ON
SPINE.

RESEARCH PAPER
ON DESK w/
TITLE & AUTHOR

VARIATION

TITLE &
INFO
UNDERNEATH...

SHELF OF
BOOK w/
TITLES

Above
Ideas vetted during the
sketching phase were then
brought to the next level as
computer-generated roughs.

Opposite, Left
By rapidly prototyping color,
type, and concepts,
Enspace was able to make quick
decisions about appropriate visual
approaches to the cover and
content sections of this book.

Tactic: Visualization

What is it?

Visualization is a rapid prototyping tool that designers use to make concepts easily understood. Visualization techniques help designers examine form, concepts, or even usability. Whether executed on paper or rendered in a three-dimensional modeling program, visualization helps make abstract ideas into concrete tangible objects.

What can it do?

Visualization can help the designer/researcher avoid potential misconceptions with both clients and members of the design team. For example, presenting competing products, or storyboards showing the client's product in context, provides others with a greater understanding of what a designer is trying to ultimately achieve. Using visualization as a part of an iterative design process allows for earlier testing and reduces the risk of going to market with a product that doesn't resonate in the market or meet the needs of the end user.

How is it used?

Designers can use a broad range of tools for visualization, including computer renderings, models, comps, storyboards and mood boards to visually articulate their concepts. Computer renderings and prototypes help communicate three-dimensional objects and environments. Storyboards or visual narratives can show how the product can be used in context. Designers can also use visual thinking or graphic organizers such as mind maps, to communicate concepts.

When is it used?

Visualization is formative research. In the early phases of the design process, rough visualization techniques such as sketching or paper prototypes are quick, cheap, and easy to execute and update based on client feedback. During later stages of the design process, refining these prototypes ensures that research findings are reflected in the end product.

Level of difficulty/complexity

Designers are by nature visual learners, and this research tactic is a component of almost all design educations, making it the most commonly used form of design research.

Opposite
KINETIK collected these visual references when developing the identity for Restaurant Kolumbia, a gourmet establishment in the heart of Washington, D.C. By gathering examples of cultural iconography, successful eatery interiors, and other restaurant marks, the KINETIK design team was able to make aesthetic decisions that positioned Restaurant Kolumbia comfortably within its price demographic while at the same time differentiating it from competitors.

Tactic: Color Theory/Color Predictions

What is it?

Color psychology studies the effects that colors have on human behavior.

What can it do?

Color is a powerful nonverbal communication tool and can play an important role in the success of commercial projects. Color can evoke emotions, elicit feelings—even cause hunger (reds and oranges have been linked to inspiring hunger and even speeding up food consumption)! Color perceptions are frequently based on shared experience and cultural association. For example warm colors such as yellow, orange, and red are linked with heat, fire, passion, love, and excitement. Cool colors such as blue, green, and violet are connected with the sea, sky, calmness, tranquility, and unity. Designers should be sensitive to the cultural perceptions of their target audience; for example, in many Western countries black is evocative of death, whereas in many non-western countries death is represented by white. When branding a product for a global market, color selections require especially close consideration.[6]

How is it used?

By studying basic color psychology and researching color trends, designers can use color to help support their concepts. Pantone, Inc.[7], provides free documentation on color forecasting every year and offers for-hire color specialization services for designers. Beyond supplying ink to printers, Pantone can help your team with color ideation and validation by doing research into target market, brand positioning, substrate suitability (Web, paper, or textile), color meanings and association, trends, and psychology. Pantone can also provide guidance on achieving consistent reproduction across varying media.

When is it used?

Decisions on color and the use of color psychology are tested during visual explorations of form. Designers can choose the most appropriate color palette for a project based on preliminary research findings that illuminate the target market and color trends.

Level of difficulty/complexity

Choosing the right color palette is essential to any design undertaking. In addition to Pantone, there are several organizations, including the Color Association of the United States[8] and the international Color Marketing Group,[9] that can be helpful when forecasting and selecting appropriate color. In addition, there are numerous books available on color theory, psychology, and palettes.

Color theory and predictions are also commonly used as a component of marketing research.

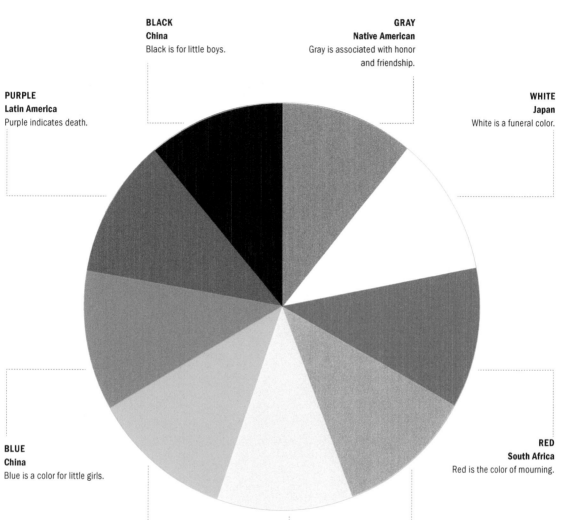

BLACK
China
Black is for little boys.

GRAY
Native American
Gray is associated with honor
and friendship.

PURPLE
Latin America
Purple indicates death.

WHITE
Japan
White is a funeral color.

BLUE
China
Blue is a color for little girls.

RED
South Africa
Red is the color of mourning.

GREEN
Islam
Green is associated with
paradise.

ORANGE
India
Orange signifies Hinduism.

YELLOW
Japan
Yellow is associated with
courage.

Above
Colors can have strong negative
or positive emotional impact. This
diagram outlines psychological
color associations from cultures
and countries around the world.

Right
A recent study done by the University of Rochester found that the number of color-sensitive cones in the human retina differs by up to forty times from person to person. Though people may claim to have common color experiences, they may not all be seeing the same thing. For example, some people may say that this pear is green, others yellow. Perceptions of color are often highly individualized.[10]

2

PRACTICING RESEARCH-DRIVEN DESIGN

RESEARCH + PROCESS

All designers are familiar with the creative process, but incorporating research methods into the practice of visual communication presents new challenges. This chapter takes a closer look at how designers integrate research and process, document their findings systematically, and articulate the value of their investigations to both clients and peers.

↓

Sometimes simple but often complex, the "process" used by graphic designers and their respective studios varies widely.

Whether the project is print, interactive, or three-dimensional in nature, designers use an established set of procedures to create innovative solutions to communication problems. Many studios offer their methods as proprietary services, noting the value that process adds in the otherwise intangible medium of creativity.

The graphic design process, as traditionally defined, is modeled around the physical creation of a single artifact: an annual report, a website, a poster, a logo, a brochure, and so on. As such, the process is inevitably project-oriented as well as linear— it starts with research and progresses through concept development, prototype, production, and delivery. Historically, the research phase begins with a review of a client's internal documents, interviews with key personnel or customers, and/or competitor analysis. These actions help a designer better understand an organization's goals and determine strategy and direction. Though these forms of preliminary research are invaluable to a project's success, they are but an early step in its creation.

Research, as defined in this book, does not merely initiate the process but rather augments it by integrating systematic investigation into each phase of a project's development. The research-driven design process also depends on assessment, or summative evaluation, which is undertaken throughout the course of (or even at the end of) a project. This allows the designer to reconsider assumptions gleaned from preliminary research. Using this data, the designer may opt to make adjustments to a design either before or, in certain situations, after production. This process of reevaluation creates a culture of consultation. As a result, research-driven designers can engage in long-term relationships with their clients, acting as strategic business partners rather than service providers assigned to singular commissions.

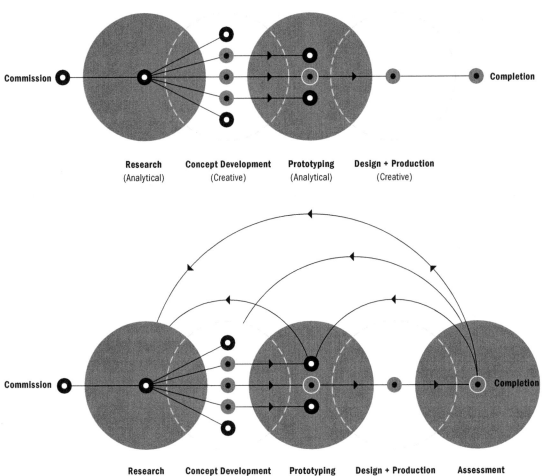

Research
(Analytical)

Concept Development
(Creative)

Prototyping
(Analytical)

Design + Production
(Creative)

Research
(Analytical)

Concept Development
(Creative)

Prototyping
(Analytical)

Design + Production
(Creative)

Assessment
(Analytical)

Top

Design is often viewed as a
linear process. It begins with
formative research—define
the problem—then progresses
through concept development,
prototype, production, and
delivery. Process, as depicted
here, focuses on the creation of
a singular artifact or campaign.

Above

Applying research methods
or data in multiple phases
of the design process allows
the designer to redefine
preliminary assumptions about
a project. While this model may
involve more iteration during
development, better-informed
design decisions more often
lead to successful outcomes.
By adding an assessment phase
to the process, the designer
can track the successes and/or
shortcomings of a project. This
summative consultation is yet
another service designers can
offer to their clients, and it may
help build ongoing relationships,
profitable to both parties.

MAPPING A
STRATEGIC DIRECTION

Graphic design researchers gather information and use those findings to solve specific visual communication problems. Because each project or commission has a unique set of goals, requirements, and budget and time constraints, it is imperative to outline a strategic direction before beginning the design process. Developing a research strategy creates a clear framework in which the designer can conduct and vet their investigation. Whether the tactics employed focus on market trends, consumer preferences, or brand perceptions, a comprehensive strategy for gathering data will help clarify both the problem to be solved and the resources necessary to accomplish project goals.

Many large design studios or advertising agencies that are already billing their clients for research services have proprietary processes—the details of which they guard closely from the competition. Numerous small firms, sole proprietors, and freelancers have also outlined research patterns, customized to their resources. Creative processes, whether proprietary or public domain, allow the designer to pair the most appropriate research tools with project requirements—without reinventing the wheel for each assignment. Individuals new to the concept of design research may find the following established processes to be an invaluable foundation on which to base their own investigations.

Above
In a manufacturing-based economy, reading, writing, and arithmetic were valuable skill sets. Workers in an information-based economy need information seeking and using strategies in addition to these primary abilities.

The Big6™ + Information Literacy

Information Literacy, a life-long learning strategy, focuses on empowering individuals by instilling the ability to recognize when information is needed and to have the skills to find, evaluate, analyze, and effectively use that information.[11] Designers will find that information literacy strategies coincide with their ability to find, harvest, and analyze complex content, creating a familiar environment for the practiced information architect.

There are numerous documented models for framing research problems. One that coalesces particularly well with the problem-solving skill sets of visual communication design is The Big6™.[12] The Big6™ is an information literacy model, or information problem-solving strategy, developed by Dr. Mike Eisenberg and Bob Berkowitz (dean of the University of Washington Information School, and school library media specialist with the Wayne Central School District in Ontario Center, New York, respectively). This model, which provides the user with a formula for problem solving, has been widely used, from educational settings to corporate professional development programs to adult retraining. Because of its inherent flexibility, the Big6™ can be used as a model for approaching any information-based problem, design projects included. Many designers will, in fact, find that they are already going through a number of the documented Big6™ steps when working on creative communication projects. Eisenberg and Berkowitz say of the Big6™: "It's not necessary to complete these stages in a linear order, and a given stage doesn't have to take a lot of time." This is especially welcome news to creatives with tight production schedules and modest budgets.

The Big6™ process uses these six steps to clarify an information-based problem. Try applying them to your next project.

1. Task Definition

   1.1 Define the information problem

   1.2 Identify information needed

2. Information Seeking Strategies

   2.1 Determine all possible sources

   2.2 Select the best sources

3. Location + Access

   3.1 Locate sources (intellectually and physically)

   3.2 Find information within sources

4. Use of Information

   4.1 Engage (e.g., read, hear, view, touch)

   4.2 Extract relevant information

5. Synthesis

   5.1 Organize from multiple sources

   5.2 Present the information

6. Evaluation

   6.1 Judge the product (effectiveness)

   6.2 Judge the process (efficiency)

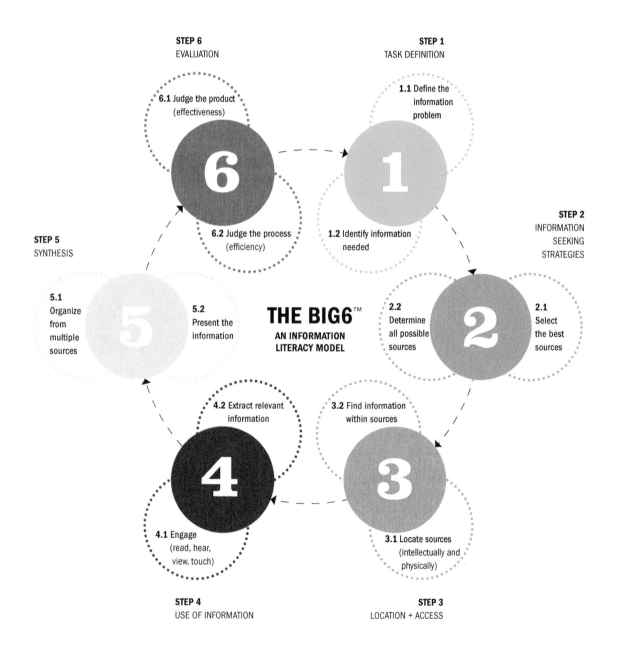

STEP 6
EVALUATION

STEP 1
TASK DEFINITION

6.1 Judge the product
(effectiveness)

1.1 Define the
information
problem

6

1

STEP 5
SYNTHESIS

6.2 Judge the process
(efficiency)

1.2 Identify information
needed

STEP 2
INFORMATION
SEEKING
STRATEGIES

5.1
Organize
from
multiple
sources

5.2
Present the
information

THE BIG6™

AN INFORMATION
LITERACY MODEL

2.2
Determine
all possible
sources

2.1
Select
the best
sources

5

2

4.2 Extract relevant
information

3.2 Find information
within sources

4

3

4.1 Engage
(read, hear,
view, touch)

3.1 Locate sources
(intellectually and
physically)

STEP 4
USE OF INFORMATION

STEP 3
LOCATION + ACCESS

AIGA's Designing Framework

↓

Designing Framework, developed by AIGA (the American Institute of Graphic Arts) may also prove a useful model, either for those seeking creative structure or for those seeking to define the power of design. Designing Framework differs from the Big6™ in that it is not intentionally an information literacy model but rather a process model developed by designers for designers. Created by AIGA to increase the understanding of design, this model showcases design thinking and outlines its role in business strategy, creative development, and value creation.[13]

AIGA's Designing Framework divides project development into three categories: defining the problem, innovating, and generating value. Each of these categories offers a series of steps that may be engaged in any order, depending on the size, scope, and purpose of the project at hand. The process is not intended to be linear and may be taken out of sequence to achieve project aims.

Especially helpful to individuals new to the concepts of design research or established creative processes, AIGA's Designing Framework is illustrated by a growing series of online case studies, submitted by individuals and firms that have successfully used this structure in professional practice.[14]

AIGA's Designing Framework is outlined below.

Defining the Problem:

· Defining the problem

· Envisioning the desired end state (knowing what victory looks like)

· Defining the approach by which victory can be achieved

· Inciting support and then action

Innovating:

· Seeking insight to inform the prototyping of the solution

· Prototyping potential solutions

· Delineating the tough choices

· Enabling the team to work as a team

Generating Value:

· Choosing the best solution, then activating it

· Making sure people know about your solution

· Selling the solution

· Rapidly learning and "tacking" based on your successes and failures

Above, Left
Commonly referred to as "the little red book" when in print form, AIGA's Designing Framework outlines a flexible process for developing creative projects, engaging in research, and promoting the value of design.

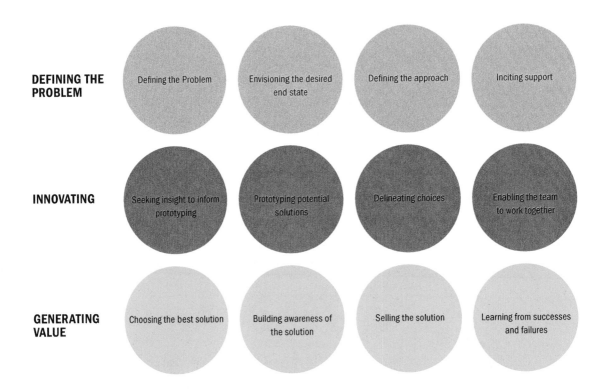

DEFINING THE PROBLEM	Defining the Problem	Envisioning the desired end state	Defining the approach	Inciting support
INNOVATING	Seeking insight to inform prototyping	Prototyping potential solutions	Delineating choices	Enabling the team to work together
GENERATING VALUE	Choosing the best solution	Building awareness of the solution	Selling the solution	Learning from successes and failures

Above
AIGA's Designing Framework breaks the creative process into three distinct categories: defining the problem, innovating, and generating value. During project development, designers may engage in multiple sub-categories, using the process in a nonlinear fashion to improve not only their end results but also their ability to promote the value of the resulting artifacts and the thinking that created them.

Below
For a more detailed explanation of AIGA's Designing Framework, view an interactive illustration of the process and browse case studies at designing.aiga.org/

Design Council Outlines The Design Process

Another applicable structure for creative development inclusive of research is The Design Process as outlined by the United Kingdom's Design Council, an organization created by the British government in 1944 to champion design. The Design Process outlines successful project development steps for creative professionals working in any field. It diagrams five stages that all designers must navigate when undertaking a commission. The Design Council suggests that this model is most functional when there is active collaboration between designer and client.

The Design Process is summarized below.[15]

First steps

· Begin with a design brief that frames the project and outlines strategic objectives.

· Ask the right questions. This is essential to writing a good brief.

· Investigate why design work is needed.

· Define the problem before working toward a solution.

Research

· Carry out research both before and during the design process.

· Focus research on the user.

· Observe customer behavior. This makes it easier to create something that fulfills a need and can also provide creative inspiration.

Planning

· Account for internal resources, people, and information.

Communication

· Make the relationship between client and designer a two-way street.

· Predetermine review stages so that the project doesn't progress in the wrong direction.

· Ensure that all parts of an organization are on board with the evolving design process.

Implementation

· Don't let designers exit the scene during implementation.

· Establish assessment procedures so that the design process can be improved in the future.

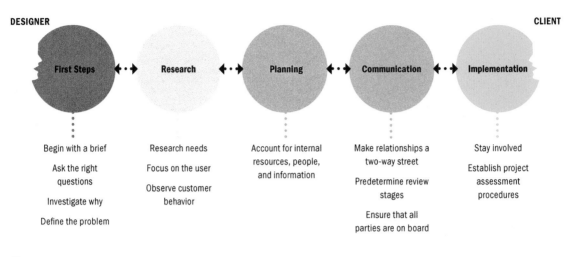

DESIGNER   **CLIENT**

First Steps	Research	Planning	Communication	Implementation

Begin with a brief

Ask the right
questions

Investigate why

Define the problem

Research needs

Focus on the user

Observe customer
behavior

Account for internal
resources, people,
and information

Make relationships a
two-way street

Predetermine review
stages

Ensure that all
parties are on board

Stay involved

Establish project
assessment
procedures

Above
The Design Process, as explained
by the Design Council, is
successful only when the creative
team participates in all steps of
project development.

TRIANGULATION:
CONFIRMING RESEARCH FINDINGS

Triangulation is the process of combining several different research methods to illuminate one area of study—in other words—using several research tools to examine the same thing. Triangulation is commonly used by the social sciences and adds credibility to qualitative research. By incorporating different tactics, the researcher can overcome issues of validity inherent with many singular qualitative approaches. The goal of triangulation is to confirm the findings of each individual tactic by focusing on where the collected information overlaps. This area of overlap, called convergence, is considered to be the most accurate representation of truth.

Research findings can be triangulated in a number of ways. For example, data triangulation would compare the results of a variety of data-gathering tactics (perhaps collected via surveys, demographics, and psychographics). Investigator triangulation would compare the findings of multiple researchers (perhaps collected via photo ethnography, visual

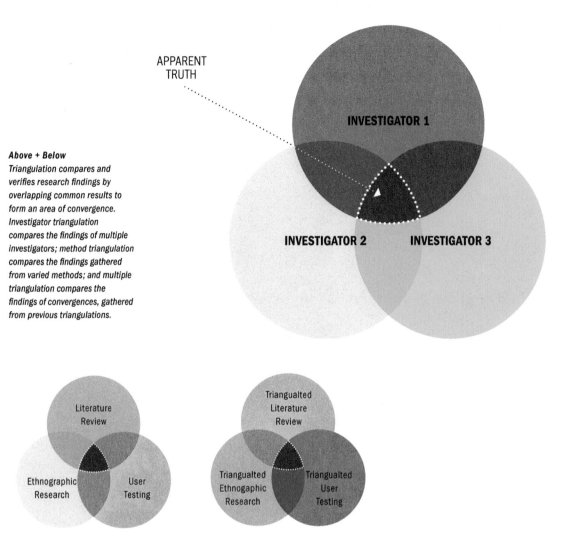

APPARENT
TRUTH

INVESTIGATOR 1

INVESTIGATOR 2   **INVESTIGATOR 3**

Above + Below
Triangulation compares and
verifies research findings by
overlapping common results to
form an area of convergence.
Investigator triangulation
compares the findings of multiple
investigators; method triangulation
compares the findings gathered
from varied methods; and multiple
triangulation compares the
findings of convergences, gathered
from previous triangulations.

Literature
Review

Ethnographic
Research

User
Testing

Triangualted
Literature
Review

Triangualted
Ethnogaphic
Research

Triangualted
User
Testing

anthropology, and observational research). Method
triangulation would compare the finding of multiple and
varied research tactics (perhaps collected via focus
groups, Web analytics, and color predictions). To be
unequivocally thorough, a researcher might employ
multiple triangulation, comparing convergences (the
results of a variety of triangulation processes).

EXPERT VOICES

Ashwini Deshpande
Founder, Director + Principal
Designer

Elephant Strategy + Design
Pune, India

Multi-Cultural Assignment, Multi-Lateral Research

In creating a retail presence for a new shampoo, we faced enormous challenges that required intensive and unique research. Our large corporate client markets everyday and luxury necessities internationally but until recently, had focused only on developed countries.

Our client was looking to tap into the endless opportunities in the markets of developing nations. They knew that the developing world buys and sells goods differently and that methods of retail communication used in modern retail are not effective in those countries. This client has presence throughout the world, so we examined buying and selling tactics in eighty prominent developing countries and found similarities in the stores across these regions.

Research helped us develop a deep understanding of the diverse cultures being examined...

Most developing markets feature small, locally run shops that have disorganized and cluttered retail displays. Beauty soap may appear next to a box of biscuits or even a pack of cigarettes. Additionally, these markets do not have a steady supply of electricity and often face extreme weather conditions.

Research helped us develop a deep understanding of the diverse cultures being examined so we could create designs that would work in a wide variety of developing regions. Our challenge was to come up with retail design solutions that would reinforce the global brand equity, answer some of the issues that our research exposed, and attract shoppers in small corner shops across all these regions.

Since the purpose of this exercise was to understand the possibilities and limitations of traditional, compact shops, an extensive photo-documentation and classification of shops across all relevant markets was required. Research was done by local client teams, our partners from the Design Alliance in Asia, and designer friends from eastern Europe, the Middle East, and Latin America.

Along with photographs, we collected some basic information about the shops. This consisted primarily of floor area, orientation, shop layouts, illumination, display space, display patterns, frequency of change, and other factors.

This research was followed by three other elements:

- **Shopper observations:** The people purchasing consumer goods in developing nations are almost always female. Our teams observed the shopper's path, focus, concerns, angle of vision, questions to the shop's staff, and the relation between her shopping list and actual purchase, as well as what she noticed first, and whether it had any impact on her purchase.

- **Cognitive interviews:** Along with a research company, our team interviewed shoppers to get insights into preferences for colors, shapes, and materials. These interviews also helped us classify the preferences of planned shoppers and impulse shoppers.

- **Focus group discussions with shop owners:** This was done with the help of a research agency. We worked with five groups of shop owners to get their understanding of shopper behavior and successful display ideas. They also provided insights on the effects of weather, certain colors, materials, shapes, maintenance of point-of-sale devices, power consumption, and other factors.

Based on our analysis of the above, Elephant came to the following conclusions:

- Product placement is crucial for the impulse shopper, whereas the planned shopper wants the product to be on the same shelf every time.

- The most crucial time to engage a shopper is when she is standing at the counter, waiting for the staff to find the product from her list.

- Anything in the line of vision during this wait is noticed and registered.

- Movement, unusual shapes, shine, glitter, shimmer, and sound attract attention.

- Although any promotion outside the shop is easily seen by passersby, the shopper may or may not notice it. When she enters the shop, she is either placing her car keys inside her bag, finding her shopping list, returning the phone call she had to miss while driving, or otherwise distracted.

- If a counter is very crowded, the shopper concentrates on her money rather than on displays.

These findings became the brief for point-of-sale and shelving devices for the shampoo brand in developing countries. Without the research, a well-defined brief could not have been achieved and, as a result, the design solutions may have been inaccurate.

Clockwise from Top Left
Morocco, Russia, Sri Lanka,
India, Turkey

Opposite
Laos

GRAPHIC ORGANIZERS:
RESEARCH FINDINGS VISUALIZED

Graphic organizers are excellent visual tools that help designers connect concepts and see the relationships between information sets. Graphic organizers can be used for a variety of purposes, such as illustrating subject associations, demonstrating a sequence of events, or comparing and contrasting concepts.

Many creatives are already familiar with the use of graphic organizers. Web and interactive designers develop flow charts as a preliminary tool to help organize information in nonlinear structures. These charts help them view the connections between chunks of information and also the navigational paths that a user may take through a website. When designing large printed documents, book maps (sometimes called content diagrams) are often used to organize information and images. These maps and diagrams also help the designer outline the pacing of the document. Beyond structuring information, graphic organizers can be used to correlate research with new ideas. Designers can use mind maps (sometimes called brainstorming maps) to connect a variety of experiences and concepts. Think of mind maps as free association visualized.

Although you may already employ graphic organizers in your practice, a simple Web search may reveal several other standard processes. Developed for researchers and educators, and ranging from downloadable worksheets[16] to software[17] to interactive tools,[18] these resources can be helpful when applied to the design process.

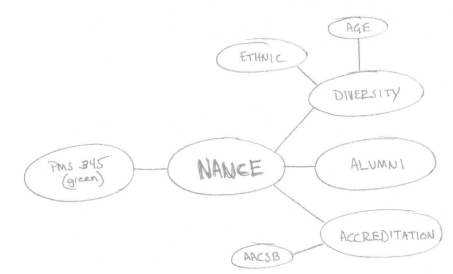

Left
Mind maps, or brainstorming maps, allow the researcher to visualize connections between information sets that were previously thought to be unrelated.

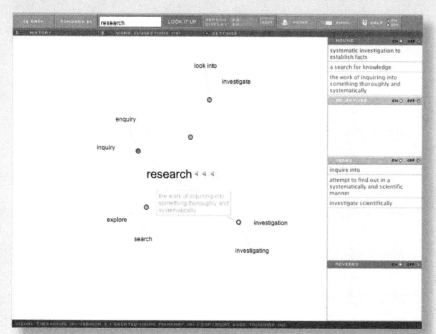

Left
ThinkLab's Visual Thesaurus uses a graphic organizer to link words and concepts visually.

K	W	H	L
What do I **know**?	**What** do I need to find out?	**How** am I going to find the information I need?	What have I **learned**?

Left
*KWHL stands for "What do we **K**now? **W**hat do we need to know? **H**ow can we find the information? What have we **L**earned?" KWHL tables can aid in developing a design project by graphing holes in the research process and suggesting how to fill them.*

Patient Journey Framework

The patient journey framework, populated by questions for each stage, suggested opportunities for the system to translate itself for the patient.

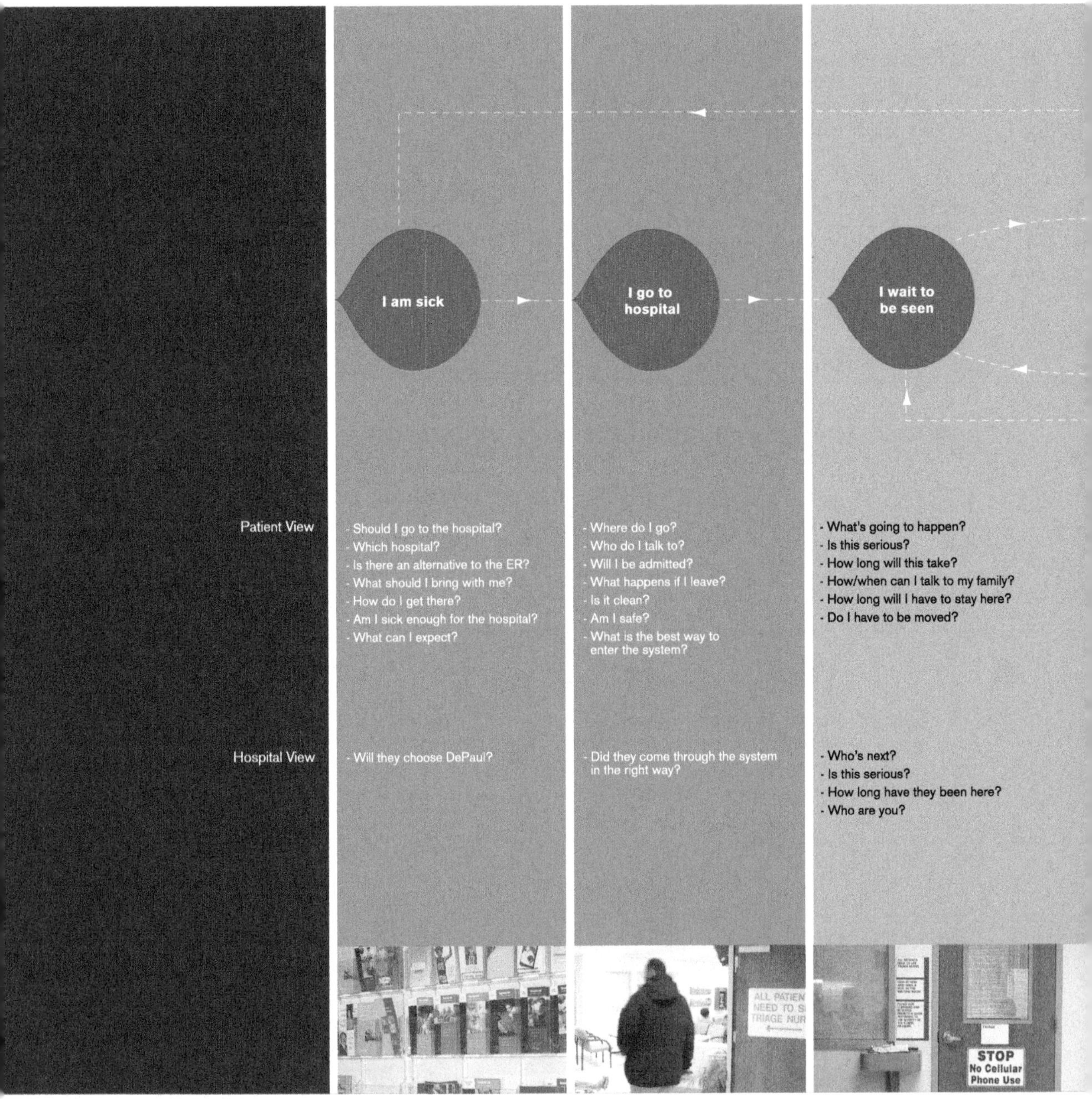

I am sick

I go to hospital

I wait to be seen

Patient View

- Should I go to the hospital?
- Which hospital?
- Is there an alternative to the ER?
- What should I bring with me?
- How do I get there?
- Am I sick enough for the hospital?
- What can I expect?

- Where do I go?
- Who do I talk to?
- Will I be admitted?
- What happens if I leave?
- Is it clean?
- Am I safe?
- What is the best way to enter the system?

- What's going to happen?
- Is this serious?
- How long will this take?
- How/when can I talk to my family?
- How long will I have to stay here?
- Do I have to be moved?

Hospital View

- Will they choose DePaul?

- Did they come through the system in the right way?

- Who's next?
- Is this serious?
- How long have they been here?
- Who are you?

Above

Event Maps can be used by designers to predetermine the sequence of user behavior in an interactive environment, forecast the desired reaction to a point of purchase display, or even predict navigation of a three-dimensional space.

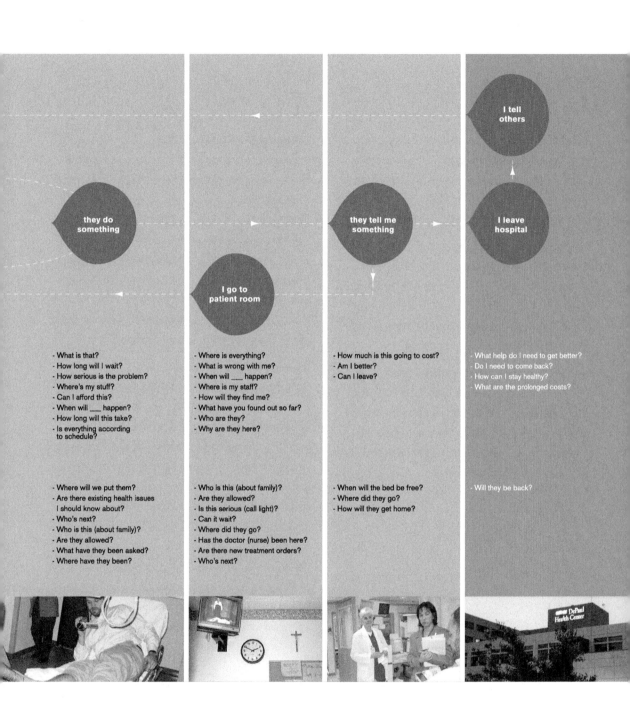

they do something

I go to patient room

they tell me something

I leave hospital

I tell others

- What is that?
- How long will I wait?
- How serious is the problem?
- Where's my stuff?
- Can I afford this?
- When will ___ happen?
- How long will this take?
- Is everything according to schedule?

- Where is everything?
- What is wrong with me?
- When will ___ happen?
- Where is my staff?
- How will they find me?
- What have you found out so far?
- Who are they?
- Why are they here?

- How much is this going to cost?
- Am I better?
- Can I leave?

- What help do I need to get better?
- Do I need to come back?
- How can I stay healthy?
- What are the prolonged costs?

- Where will we put them?
- Are there existing health issues I should know about?
- Who's next?
- Who is this (about family)?
- Are they allowed?
- What have they been asked?
- Where have they been?

- Who is this (about family)?
- Are they allowed?
- Is this serious (call light)?
- Can it wait?
- Where did they go?
- Has the doctor (nurse) been here?
- Are there new treatment orders?
- Who's next?

- When will the bed be free?
- Where did they go?
- How will they get home?

- Will they be back?

DOCUMENTATION
OF RESEARCH

↓

Clear documentation in all stages of the research process allows for rapid analysis, application, and dissemination of research findings. By developing a method for careful cataloging of research, the process is both more efficient and more accurate.

Though designers are not required to publish their research in a traditional sense, as scientists and academics are, they do present their findings to the client. Proper documentation will allow the client to understand how conclusions have been made and provide insight into aesthetic directions.

Beyond presenting research to clients, designers may wish to publish their projects in a public forum. Documentation of the research undertaken to meet project demands is a valuable tool for raising the perceived value of visual communication design and the expertise of its practitioners.

Developmental Documentation

It is essential to record and organize your research clearly. To get the most out of the investigative process, designers should take copious notes, organizing them into categories, and keeping them in a job ticket of some kind. Though this may sound like elementary advice, thorough documentation during the creative process is necessary in order to share your research with either the client or other members of the creative team. These collections are valuable resources should any of your findings come under scrutiny.

Cumulative Documentation

Once a project has been completed and delivered to the client, research is almost over. Documenting the functionality and success of a finished project is an important phase in the research cycle and should not be overlooked. Often, these kinds of statistics are the most compelling when making a case for the value of design. Additionally, designers and their respective studios can learn important lessons by reflecting on specific achievements and failures during a project's development. Clients may be asked to contribute a letter or fill out a questionnaire describing their experience and level of satisfaction with the finished project. This appraisal should be documented in an internal case study and used to streamline future assignments.

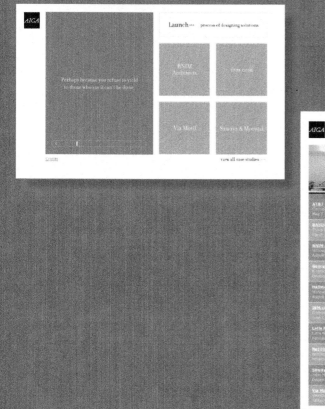

Case Studies

Contribute your case study >>>

1	2	3	4	5	6	7	8	9	10	11	12

why

BNIM

View other steps for this project:
why 5 6 9

PROJECT GOAL
Develop a brand identity that positions BNIM as a leader in
creating responsible, sustainable design for the future.

PROJECT BACKGROUND
In business for more than 30 years, BNIM is ranked among
the top architectural firms in the Midwest and one of the
pioneers in sustainable design in the U.S. In an initiative to
further stimulate innovation and build credibility as an
expert in sustainable/renewable design, BNIM established
five independent studios. To support these changes, BNIM
needed an identity and communications plan that reflected
their commitment to both urban development and their
nationally known dedication to responsible, sustainable
design practices.

Steps for this project:

5   6   9

Submitted by:
Willoughby Design Group

Date:
January, 2003

Client Name:
BNIM Architects

Project Name:
Brand Identity

Date Started:
August, 2000

Date Completed:
December, 2000

Duration of Project:
b weeks

Project Team:

Ann Willoughby
Creative Overview

Deb Tagtalianidis
Creative Director

Nicole Satterwhite
Art Director

Above, Left
*AIGA members can document
their use of Designing Framework
by publishing case studies on
AIGA's website to share with the
design community. This Web
resource provides good reference
material for both designers and
design buyers and also serves as
publicity for participants. Other
design organizations around the
world offer similar opportunities
on their websites, so be sure to
see what is available in your area.*

Personal Research Morgues

Build your own library: By documenting and archiving research and processes and creating case studies of past projects, designers can start to build their own research library. Secondary research done for new projects does not always have to come exclusively from outside sources. Research undertaken for one project may also be valuable for later commissions. By archiving research and creative processes, documenting learning outcomes, showcasing end products, and understanding how they work, the designer can build a proprietary body of knowledge, which will be invaluable for soliciting and retaining future work.

Contributing to a Body of Knowledge

Build your profession: Publishing successful research-driven projects—either individually or through organizations such as AIGA, the Design Management Institute, the Design Council, or ICOGRADA—contributes to the collective body of knowledge in the field and promotes the undeniable value of design.

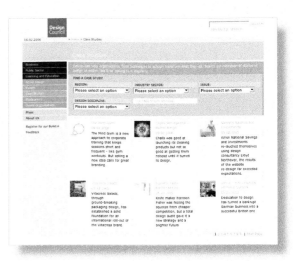

Top
Published through the Harvard Business School, the Design Management Institute (DMI) has built an extensive library of case studies showcasing the impact design has on business and industry. Because of their connection to the revered Harvard Business School, these case studies make a particularly effective case for the value of design when shared with clients or other potential design buyers.

Above
The Design Council regularly publishes case studies on their website to promote the value design creates. These juried submissions are organized by geographic location, industry, discipline, or issue, allowing readers to quickly locate the information they are seeking.

ARTICULATING VALUE

↓

Cultivating an environment conducive to research investigations is an important step in every designer's professional development. Research—the key to aiming creative impulses properly—provides the designer with documentation supporting aesthetic/design decisions. Clearly articulating the relevance of research and process is essential—resulting in both time and budgetary allowances for proper investigation and project development.

Subjectivity Finds Context

By nature, designers are visual people. They have years of training dedicated to communicating with an external audience through the use of typography, color, and imagery. They often understand intuitively what it takes to create attention-grabbing artifacts that delight, inform, or inspire. However, designers speak an industry-specific language, and when working directly with clients—the majority of whom went to business school—they may not only find themselves up against a language barrier but against a difference of aesthetic principles as well. "Taste" is subjective, and no one will admit that they don't have any. Thus designers often find themselves explaining aesthetic decisions with formal design or typographic principles. Clients may well view these choices as arbitrary (remember, they don't know the difference between Helvetica and Arial). When documented research has been used to

Above, Following Page
Color Forecasting tools generated by Pantone can help designers pinpoint color choices for specific markets, industries, and client needs.

The images above show fall 2006 interior and fashion design color forecasts. Graphic designers can often find color cues in sister industries.

help guide the creative process, however, the designer will experience more success validating their work. For example, if the Pantone Institute was commissioned to do color choice validation as primary research, the designer could point to that expert report (read: investment) to justify their color selections.

Proving Value: The U.K.'s Design Index

As budgets tighten, clients are demanding more qualitative and quantitative data to address the projected successes of marketing and design endeavors. Although in recent years design has been recognized as strategically important to fiscal success, with business innovators such as Tom Peters singing its praises, abundant "proof" supporting investments in the design process is still lacking. Enter the British Design Council. In an ongoing study this advocacy group has linked the strategic use of design to stock performance. Called the Design Index, this investigation discovered that the share prices of companies who invest in design performed up to three times better than the FTSE 100, the 100 largest companies listed on the London Stock Exchange (over the course of a recent two-year study). The original Design Index report also showed that share prices for a group of more than 150 companies recognized as effective users of design outperformed the stock market by 200 percent between 1994 and 2003.[19]

Many clients understand design as a point of differentiation but are still mystified by the creative process or unclear on the difference between aesthetic appropriateness and "taste." Today's successful designer must be able to articulate concepts familiar to business people, in order to frame communication solutions in language their client can understand. By making informed decisions—based on extensive research instead of intuitive best guesses—the designer legitimizes their professional practice and defines the power of the artifacts they create.

Legend:
- Design Portfolio
- Emerging Portfolio
- FTSE 100
- FTSE All-Share

INDICES	Number of Companies	Design Portfolio High Feb 28, 2000*	Emerging Portfolio High Dec 29, 2004*	Largest One Week Fall Sept 10, 2001*	Bear Market Low March 3, 2003*
ABSOLUTE PERFORMANCES					
FTSE 100	100	+89.8%	+40.8%	+39.1%	+2.1%
FTSE All-Share	700+	+85.3%	+43.3%	+26.5%	+0.2%
Design Index	63	+295.9%	+258.5%	+168.7%	+135.6%
Emerging Index	103	+235.0%	+281.9%	+121.1%	+110.2%
RELATIVE TO FTSE 100					
Design Index	63	+206.2%	+217.7%	+129.6%	+133.4%
Emerging Index	103	+145.2%	+241.0%	+81.9%	+108.1%
RELATIVE TO FTSE ALL-SHARE					
Design Index	63	+210.7%	+215.2%	+142.2%	+135.4%
Emerging Index	103	+149.8%	+238.6%	+94.6%	+110.0%

* All figures relative to start date of Design and Emerging Indices (December 29, 1993)

Above, Previous Page

Created by the Design Council, the Design and Emerging Indexes are groups of companies that have an award-winning history of using design effectively (Design Index hosting the most award-winning firms). These diagrams show the performance of both the Design Index and the Emerging Index as compared to the performance of the FTSE 100 and the FTSE All Share (measuring major capital and industry segments of the U.K. market) over a ten-year period. Both the Design Index and the Emerging Index outpaced the FTSE 100 and the FTSE All Share by more than 200 percent over the duration of the study.

TAILORING
RESEARCH
METHODOLOGY

3

A PERFECT FIT

All designers face similar challenges when incorporating research into their creative process—whether they are students, educators, freelancers, or part of a creative team. What differs for each is access to and availability of resources. This chapter provides examples of how to tailor the methods reviewed in Chapter One to fit almost any need, time frame, or budget.

RESEARCH FOR STUDENT DESIGNERS

The goal of all design research is to empower the designer to make informed decisions and then to provide support for their aesthetic rationale. In the case of student work, project scope and limited resources often force research practices to be more informal. Students can, however, use a number of methodologies to inform their decisions from assignment to assignment—ultimately honing their professional skills for the job market. Here are a number of ways that design students can use research practices to better inform their design solutions.

Literature Review

The term "literature review" is fairly self-explanatory: gather all materials relevant to your subject. For many students, research begins and ends online. Though the Internet is a powerful tool, the academic library is one of the best places to go for books, academic journals, newspapers, magazines, and manuscripts from professional conferences. A university library also offers access to many tools that are not readily available to the general public, such as proprietary research portals, inter-university databases, and graduate dissertations. Furthermore, trained professionals are available to assist patrons with their research efforts. Starting a project is often the hardest part. But conducting a literature review will offer valuable insight into your subject matter and better prepare you for framing the problem to be solved.

Marketing Research

Though students may lack the resources to conduct their own marketing research, they can gain much by reviewing the results of previously published marketing studies relating to their current project. Most colleges and universities have business libraries with specific access to this research. Taking the time to read and understand this type of secondary data can help focus the design process and provide statistics to support aesthetic choices. There are many online resources for free market data, including those provided by state and national governments. In the United States, for instance, the U.S. Department of Labor website (www.dol.gov) offers a great deal of data on specific industries and occupations. Outside of the United States, similar information can be found though governmental labor agencies.

Visual Exploration

As we tell all of our students: sketch! The sketching phase is a critical step in the design process and can lead to truly innovative and creative solutions. Though students' design abilities mature and they develop their own methodology for visualization, pencil and paper remain highly effective tools. Sketching allows designers to prototype concepts rapidly without being influenced by technology—so they are focused on solving the problem first and fabricating the solution second. Additionally, sitting down with a sketchbook naturally allows some time for brainstorming, forcing designers to really think about what they're trying to solve.

28 Nutritional Science

With the acquisition of Aventis Corporation, the Bayer Crop Science subgroup is one of the world's leading innovative enterprises in crop protection, seeds, bio-technology, and non-agricultural pest control. We are using our technology to enhance the quality and quantity of crops.

29 Nutritional Science

LEVITRA

Longer Lasting And Fewer Side Effects

Safer For People With Heart Problems

EXPERT
VOICES

Tips for Working with a Research Librarian

Academic librarians typically have subject specialties and professional experience that can be beneficial to students of all levels. Many librarians hold advanced degrees in their field of specialty. The following tips can help you use librarians as resources:

Dan Overfield
Business Librarian

Villanova University
Philadelphia, Pennsylvania, USA

- Don't hesitate to ask a question. A librarian's job is to connect you with the information that you need. They work to select books, magazines, journals, and databases to match the curriculum. Answering your questions is part of a librarian's daily routine.

- Questions (called reference interviews) are considered confidential. The librarian will not share the details of your question or the reasons for asking it with anyone else.

- If you pay college tuition, you owe it to yourself not to "Google" your degree. Do not cheapen your education. Libraries have access to expensive and legitimate scholarly resources that are not available elsewhere.

- An academic librarian is like a tour guide for a hike in the jungle. He or she can walk you through thousands of journals and millions of bits of information until you find exactly what you need.

You owe it to yourself not to "Google" your degree.

- If you are working on an assignment, there is a good chance that you are not alone. Save yourself (and the librarian) a lot of time by asking where to begin or continue your research. Chances are one of your classmates just asked the same question.

- Libraries use many of the same information sources as major businesses, law firms, governments, journalists, and other professionals. A librarian can teach you how to get the most from these tools and provide you with a skill that will impress future employers.

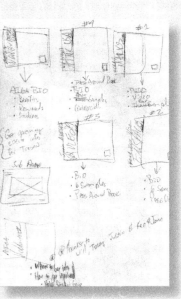

Above + Left
Gary Rozanc, an MFA student
at the University of Arizona,
used extensive sketching and
visualization tools in these AIGA
student-group promotional
posters. By articulating ideas
both visually and verbally, Rozanc
was able to execute a series that
was conceptually driven and
consistent in its presentation.

RESEARCH FOR
DESIGN EDUCATORS

In the academic arena, research can mean many things to many people. For the purposes of this book, we're discussing the application of research methods to inform and enhance student assignments. Though an emphasis on research may seem like a pedagogical shift for many design educators, it instead augments what is already being taught in the classroom during the study of form, color, typography, and communication. By integrating research methods into all levels of study, students develop a better understanding of the communications issues they are trying to solve. Research also helps designers forecast how the target audience will use artifacts they build and enables designers to articulate how their design skills create value.

In addition to the tactics outlined specifically for students in the previous section, design educators can also use the process described in the following section to bring research methods to the classroom.

Observational Research + User Testing

Observational research can be an effective way for students to gather unique information. It can also impart essential note-taking and organizational skills. For example, when assigning an interactive project, require students to observe users navigating beta versions. By documenting behavior, the student will be better able to address user needs and adjust the interface and information architecture accordingly. Many universities have developed usability labs, often housed in computer science or information technology departments, providing an interdisciplinary opportunity for collaboration. In addition, this kind of audience test might be the first exposure a student has to critical feedback, aside

from that offered by instructors or peers. Thus this process adds both a valuable tactic and a real-world client experience to the student's growing cache.

Information Literacy + Process

Educators should also emphasize the importance of information literacy. This is particularly important as visual communication design programs go beyond their foundations in fine art and align their curriculum with communication, information, and marketing studies. The ability to recognize when information is needed and to find, analyze, and apply that information is now an essential life and work skill.

The Big6™ (discussed in more detail in Chapter Two) is an information literacy model and a fantastic resource when considering how to integrate research into the classroom. As a strategy for gathering and synthesizing information, primary, secondary, and higher educators have used the Big6. It helps students determine what research methods they need to solve class projects. The design educator can then ask students to use this process as a framework for each assignment and have them record their experiences in each phase. Extensive documentation of how the Big6 has been used in teaching environments is available online[20], enabling design educators to tailor these concepts to their own objectives.

EXPERT VOICES

Using Research to Support Basic Meaning:
The Semantic Differential

It's my belief that research with viewers should not be reserved solely for upper-level undergraduate courses or graduate studies. In fact, my colleagues and I feel that it's imperative for beginning students to realize that they are creating visual form to transmit meaning and that someone will always interpret the message that they've constructed. With that goal in mind, I include the following assignment as part of an introductory visual communication design practices course.

Paul J. Nini
Professor + Visual Communication Design Undergraduate Program Coordinator

The Ohio State University Columbus, Ohio, USA

Students are asked to choose a pair of opposing concepts to visualize, such as the example provided that shows representations of "organic" and "synthetic." Students are asked to consider issues of color, form, and composition, and to use them in contrasting ways for each representation. Initial concepts are developed with cut paper and used for viewer-testing purposes. No words labeling the representations appear in these prototypical versions.

Each representation is then shown to twenty randomly selected viewers, who are asked to complete a semantic differential survey form and rank the particular concept with five associated words and their opposites. Students then display average viewer responses to the desired attributes for each representation (see chart, opposite). Responses to representations that properly convey the intended properties naturally fall to the appropriate side of the scale. Students also consider any written responses from viewers while refining their compositions, and then create final versions on the computer, where the original concept words are then added as labels.

This project introduces the basic process of defining objectives for their efforts, creating and testing a visual message, and refining that message based on viewer response, giving beginning students a glimpse of a viewer-centered research approach.[21]

Opposite
Professor Paul Nini of the Ohio State University uses survey research in intro-level courses. In this example, students test their illustration (without any typographic clues) on twenty random people. Viewers then fill out a semantic differential scale survey that can either validate the student's communication success or offer insight into improvements.

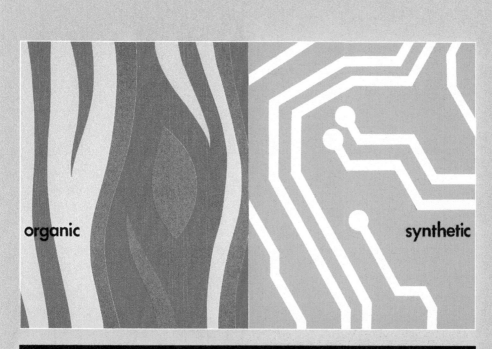

organic

synthetic

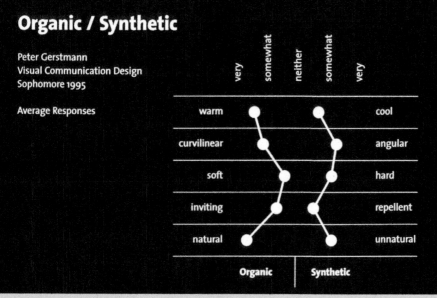

Organic / Synthetic

Peter Gerstmann
Visual Communication Design
Sophomore 1995

Average Responses

	very	somewhat	neither	somewhat	very	
warm		●		●		cool
curvilinear		●		●		angular
soft			● ●			hard
inviting			●	●		repellent
natural	●				●	unnatural
	Organic			Synthetic		

RESEARCH FOR
PRACTICING PROFESSIONALS

Small firms face many of the same challenges as freelancers or sole proprietors. Project deadlines are always tight, resources stretched too thin. They may well recognize the value of a research-driven approach but worry that conducting this kind of thorough investigation will be too costly or time consuming. Though engaging in a systematic process of information gathering may seem like yet another demand on the studio's time, it can ultimately speed up time-to-market and focus aesthetic development.

Designers who do excellent research will not waste time pursuing directions that are not viable, and the team will have qualitative or quantitative documentation validating their aesthetic choices. This will save valuable time during the client approval process. Research can provide another billable service and modify business roles from designer to design consultant. In addition to the tools previously outlined for students and educator use, any of the methods discussed in the first two chapters can be tailored to fit the needs of small firms or individuals. Here are some examples to get you started.

Color + Visualization

There are a number of resources—from expensive to open source—that can provide color guidance to the designer. Pantone, Inc., an industry leader, offers several professional services and can be retained to assist with color ideation and color validation, as well as application across media (from Web to print to textile to manufacturing). Designers can also join professional associations, such as the Color Marketing Group, that are focused on color and its application to the world of visual communication. On an annual basis, *Communication Arts* magazine profiles color trends for the upcoming year. Design powerhouse IDEO has developed the Web Color Visualizer, which allows the user to compare Web-safe color combinations applied to text and backgrounds in the click of a mouse. This tool can be used when browsing their website.[22] Color Schemer offers a range of current schemes, along with software and free online tools for selecting color palettes.[23]

Competitor Analysis

Designers should familiarize themselves immediately with a client's corporate literature at the outset of a project. Reviewing the literature of the competition can be helpful as well. Information about the competitor's brand, messaging, and media strategy are all useful. Valuable insight can be gained by determining where

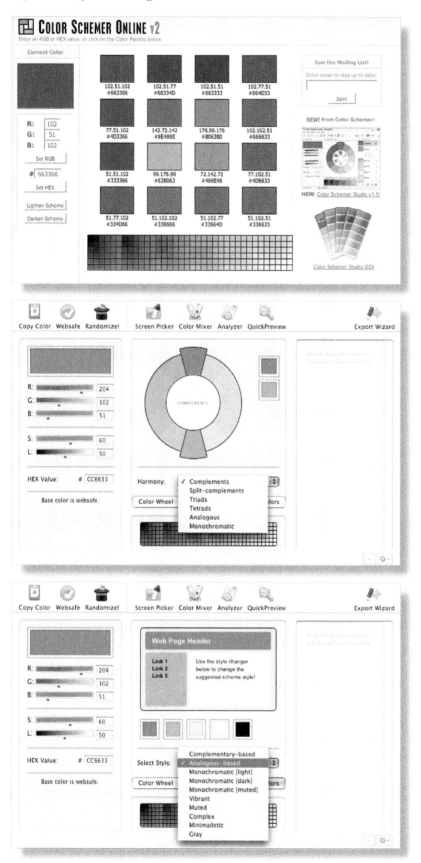

Left

Color Schemer is a small software company that creates color ideation tools for print and Web designers. Beyond the tools that they offer for sale, the company's website provides an online color palette gallery and an interactive tool that creates color schemes out of Web-safe colors.

Below

You can learn a lot from something seemingly commonplace. For example, this media kit for Dwell magazine provides demographic information about its viewing audience. Though a secondary source, this data could help assemble personas or even aid in competitor analysis. Media kits can be requested directly from the publisher, but many journals, including Dwell, also provide reader/subscriber profiles on their websites.

the competition is allocating marketing dollars. For example, if a competitor is advertising in a particular magazine, call that journal and ask for a media kit. This kit will provide demographic information about the magazine's distribution, as well as a financial breakdown of advertising costs—perhaps revealing the competition's target focus.

Marketing Research

Partnering with a market research firm to conduct primary demographic or psychographic research can prove to be a valuable investment. Information gathered here, when paired with other research tools, will provide objective and accurate data on the target audience for the project. If timelines or budgets do not allow for outsourcing primary demographic or psychographic research, a great deal of data may be collected from secondary sources. Often, corporations have employed these investigations for alternate purposes and have the data archived. Be sure to ask your client for access to any relevant statistical documentation. For example, a social services client may have conducted demographic research for a ballot issue—this same information might also be relevant to the thematic direction and design of their annual report.

Ethnographic Research

To be most effective, design firms or freelancers should work with trained ethnographers who have the professional background to interpret their observations and interviews objectively. Should financial constraints preclude partnering with an ethnographer, small firms can send members of their team out to do field research. Then triangulate the notes, observations, and interviews of each individual to determine apparent truths. Previous ethnographic studies of common subjects can also be reviewed. This secondary research may be a part of the literature review process.

Above

For this extensive corporate identity project, Eleven19 partnered with MarketCapture, a company specializing in software marketing strategy and execution. Information gathered in the formative phase of the project went on to influence the design of magazine ads, direct mail, tradeshow booth and handouts, website, email newsletters, online seminars, data sheets, case studies, and software packaging.

Above, Previous Page

When working on a rebrand for Genz-Ryan, a 50-year-old, family-run plumbing, heating, and cooling business, Catalyst Studios' budget was too tight to engage focus groups or surveys. Instead, they sought statistical information about their audience on the Web. Interviews with the Genz-Ryan staff also provided a historical overview of past successes and failures, even outlining customer complaints and perceived competitor strengths and weaknesses. This insight helped the design team to develop an extensive campaign that was both effective and award-winning.

EXPERT VOICES

Mike Bond
Director of Bond and Coyne
Associates + Senior Lecturer in
Graphic Design

Kingston University, London, UK

Approaching + Reacting to Research

Design is about understanding.

The graphic designer must have empathy for whom and for what they are designing. Building research into the design process avoids resultant design solutions serving only to satisfy the designer or to paint over the cracks of an issue.

In many ways, designers have to become mini-experts in all that they deal with to really understand the subject matter and the audience to whom they are speaking. Research in this respect is essential in getting designers to understand worlds they may not inhabit: worlds that present the designer with unfamiliar environments, scenarios, people, industries, languages, and traditions.

Research is needed to understand a client, the people they wish to communicate with, and the reasons behind the need for communication—in other words, the problem. Research should also be employed to aid the generation of visual directions and solutions.

Research should cover at least two strands at any given time. One strand provides a scenario and potentially a surface on which to work, the other provides a visual language to employ. Together they present the designer with a means to engage. Although either strand should influence the other, they are not interdependent and usually require separate and distinct approaches.

In my experience as a director of design consultancy Bond and Coyne Associates and as a lecturer at Kingston University, London, it is not so much the kind of research that is carried out as it is the designer's ability to spot the value in their research and have the confidence to react to it. That being said, there is also a danger that research can "dry-out" a solution. Research, if handled incorrectly, can take away the chance of surprise.

Therefore, the design process—and for that matter, the design studio—should allow for the unconventional to work in tandem with the methodical. Creation of project spaces in which observations, quotes, and facts are displayed in a nonlinear fashion enables the designer to get an instant overview of a situation and make connections between findings. It also allows designers to present interim thoughts and findings to others in the design team and perhaps even the client. Presenting research in this way can aid analysis while not alienating those less familiar with the design process.

Research is needed to understand a client, the people they wish to communicate with, and the reasons behind the need for communication.

Literally sit these findings alongside inspirational (perhaps image-led) research to inform possible solutions, and you have the potential for sparks of ingenuity to fly and opportunities for innovation to be spotted.

Research is kept fluid and reactions to it free-flowing as long as there is a culture (particularly in the initial stages of analysis) of "anything goes." Deferring judgment in this way helps designers build confidence in their research processes and gives them the ability to stand back, get the bigger picture, and synthesize their data without fear of being "wrong."

Remember...

- Designers need to use research as something to react against as well as respond to.

- Research should back up thinking. Making assumptions and ignorance can be the death of successful and inspiring design.

- Whenever possible, research should inform the brief in the first place, before informing the solution. People or situations cannot ask for what they do not know is possible or do not realize is necessary.

- Don't let research kill a potential idea—let it feed and support it.

- Frame the creative process with logic, and the less-expected nuances can thrive within it.

PART TWO:
RESEARCH AT WORK

4

CASE
STUDIES

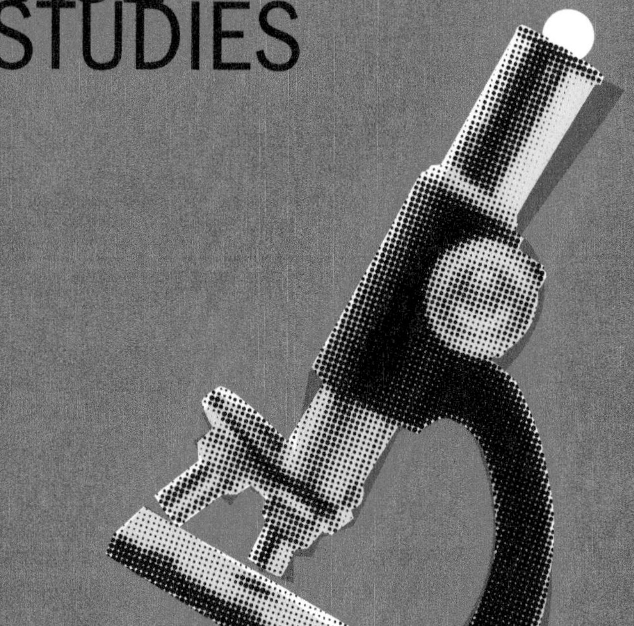

PROJECT:
Election Design:
Models for Improvement

CLIENT:
Design for Democracy

INTENDED AUDIENCE:
election officials, election-related manufacturers and printers, public officials, design educators and students, professional designers, voters

CREDITS:
Design for Democracy: Marcia Lausen and Elizabeth Tunstall, Ph.D. (For a complete list of contributors, visit the Design for Democracy website at designfordemocracy.org)

AN UNFRAMED PROBLEM

After the closely contested U.S. presidential election of 2000, leaders of the American Institute of Graphic Arts (AIGA) sought to improve ballot design. The AIGA established the Design for Democracy initiative to create a more user-centered experience. Officials hope this, in turn, will increase the participation in and accuracy of the democratic process.

Design for Democracy was not commissioned to undertake this project, but to address it proactively. "We were not asked to solve a problem—we forced ourselves upon one," says Marcia Lausen, information design director for the initiative and director of the School of Art and Design at the University of Illinois at Chicago.

"We were not asked to solve a problem, we forced ourselves upon one."

The group engaged Sapient, a leading business consultant and technology services firm, to determine voters' needs. Sapient's preliminary research, conducted pro bono, found that redesigning the ballot was only the first step toward developing a more precise election process. The research revealed opportunities for design-driven improvement in all phases of the election process.

Framing the Solution

Design for Democracy used several research tactics to frame the issues pertaining to voter experience. All of the research is classified as ethnographic, according to

Above
The "vote!" logo is a core component of the Design for Democracy initiative. Created to illustrate the positive qualities inherent in the American voting experience, the logo is freely available in both English and Spanish for use by any election authority.

Below
Research conducted by Sapient for Design for Democracy identified five different types of voters and outlined their individual motivations.

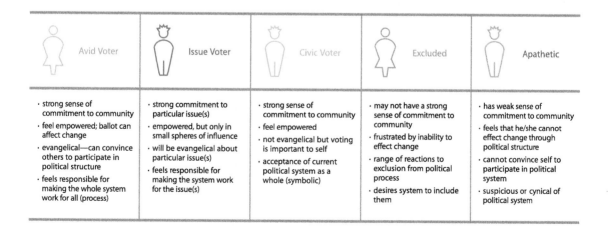

Avid Voter	Issue Voter	Civic Voter	Excluded	Apathetic
· strong sense of commitment to community · feel empowered; ballot can affect change · evangelical—can convince others to participate in political structure · feels responsible for making the whole system work for all (process)	· strong commitment to particular issue(s) · empowered, but only in small spheres of influence · will be evangelical about particular issue(s) · feels responsible for making the system work for the issue(s)	· strong sense of commitment to community · feel empowered · not evangelical but voting is important to self · acceptance of current political system as a whole (symbolic)	· may not have a strong sense of commitment to community · frustrated by inability to effect change · range of reactions to exclusion from political process · desires system to include them	· has weak sense of commitment to community · feels that he/she cannot effect change through political structure · cannot convince self to participate in political system · suspicious or cynical of political system

Lausen. Ethnography uses qualitative research, derived from observation, to explain how cultural experiences form individuals' perspectives. As a part of the study, the creative team conducted literature reviews of print and electronic election materials. The group scrutinized voter registration cards, ballots, administrative materials, voter education materials, polling place signage, and vote-by-mail programs. They supplemented this literature review by conducting personal interviews with and distributing surveys and questionnaires to election officials, voters, poll workers, and postal employees. Volunteers also observed and documented voter behavior at polling places, and the team held a mock election to witness how contextual elements can affect the voter experience.

Of the many research methods employed, Lausen found the "visual stories" method most useful. To create visual stories, UIC students and volunteers distributed logbooks and disposable cameras to voters and potential voters. Participants answered questions in the logbook, illustrated their answers with photos, and returned the materials to the designers for review.

Design for Democracy also tapped local election officials to help designers overcome the challenges of design in elections. "As a designer, it is easy to point to an illegible ballot and point out what is wrong," says Lausen. "It is a far different matter to understand the political, legal, procedural, and administrative issues that will make improvements possible. Without the involvement, cooperation, and support of election officials, our intended audience of U.S. voters would be unreachable."

Measured Success

This intense focus on research led to materials that not only improved the act of voting but also improved the entire voting process—for both voters and poll workers. Design for Democracy's efforts to clarify the democratic process in Cook County, Illinois, had dramatic results, evidenced by a 20-percent rise in participation at the polls.[24]

Research was a vital component of the design process. "Although our before-and-after images that demonstrate design improvements are powerful and compelling, this is not a world where design speaks for itself," Lausen said. "Research results have been highly influential in our path from local to national influence."

That influence has extended outward from greater Chicago, across the country— and even as far as Europe.[25]

ease of the experience

registration: easy

· long-term residents
· reside in small "villages" where they are already known (residency as well as political views)
· are already civic-minded

voting: accessible

· lives within walking distance or has cars to drive to the polls before or after work
· just asked for name and address at the polling place
· always double checks ballots to assure that their ballot will count
· verification process finds the error to be the judge's, not the voter's

getting info: unreliable

· lack of information (especially about local issues)
· too much information
· deals with the inconsistent nature of sources by using a variety: newspapers, TV, Internet, etc.

monitoring: insufficient

· lack of instant feedback telling the voter that the selection they made was for the candidate they intended
· lack of feedback telling the voter where the ballot finally goes
· time lag before local results are made known

JUDICIAL RETENTION CIRCUIT COURT
RETENCION JUDICIAL CORTE DE CIRCUITO

| Carole Kamin Bellows | YES 229 → |
| | NO 230 → |

vote yes or no
vote si o no

| David G. Lichtenstein | YES 233 → |
| | NO 234 → |

YES: Retain
the candidate in office
as Judge of the Circuit Court,
Cook County Judicial Circuit.

YES: Retenga
al candidato en su puesto
como Juez De La Corte De Circuito,
Circuito Judicial Del Condado
De Cook.

| Michael J. Hogan | YES 237 → |
| | NO 238 → |

| Alan J. Greiman | YES 241 → |
| | NO 242 → |

NO: Don't retain
the candidate in office
as Judge of the Circuit Court,
Cook County Judicial Circuit.

| Mary Maxwell Thomas | YES 245 → |
| | NO 246 → |

NO: No retenga
al candidato en su puesto
como Juez De La Corte De Circuito,
Circuito Judicial Del Condado
De Cook.

| Francis Barth | YES 249 → |
| | NO 250 → |

| Stuart Allen Nudelman | YES 253 → |
| | NO 254 → |

| Edward R. Burr | YES 257 → |
| | NO 258 → |

| Barbara J. Disko | YES 261 → |
| | NO 262 → |

Official Ballot
Balota Oficial

G

JUDICIAL RETENTION CIRCUIT COURT
RETENCION JUDICIAL CORTE DE CIRCUITO

| ← 231 YES | Kathy M. Flanagan |
| ← 232 NO | |

vote yes or no
voto si o no

| ← 235 YES | Curtis Heaston |
| ← 236 NO | |

| ← 239 YES | Michael J. Kelly |
| ← 240 NO | |

| ← 243 YES | John E. Morrissey |
| ← 244 NO | |

| ← 247 YES | Ronald C. Riley |
| ← 248 NO | |

| ← 251 YES | Francis X. Golniewicz |
| ← 252 NO | |

If you spoil your ballot,
ask the judge for a new one.
Si usted daña su balota,
pídale una balota nueva al Juez.

| ← 255 YES | Moshe Jacobius |
| ← 256 NO | |

| ← 259 YES | Stuart F. Lubin |
| ← 260 NO | |

Turn page to continue voting.
Voltee la página para continuar
votando.

| ← 263 YES | Marvin P. Luckman |
| ← 264 NO | |

15

Top
Examination of the voting process identified four phases: registering, getting information, voting, and monitoring choices. Mapping the voter archetypes through this process, Sapient uncovered obstacles in each phase.

Above
The focus of information design is to create unambiguous communications. Design for Democracy's version of the Cook County butterfly ballot is evidence that design can improve access to complex information.

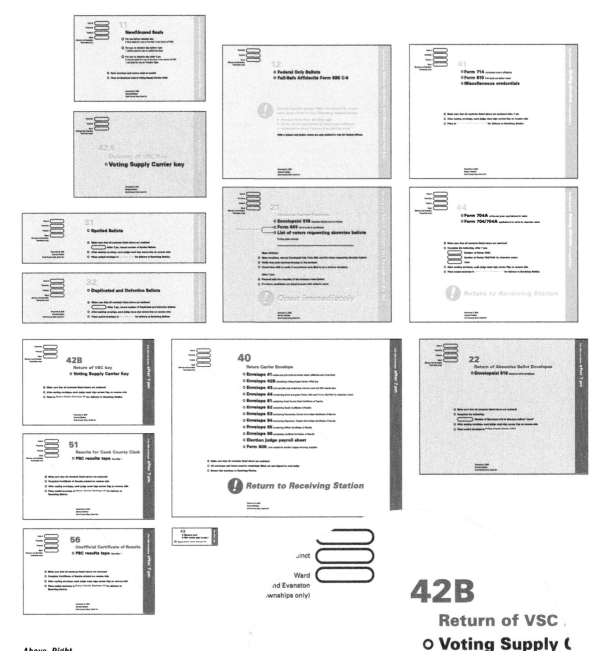

Above, Right
Materials used by poll workers
for record keeping and vote
recording can be confusing.
This document management
system was developed to clarify
the process by using large
reference numbers, consistent
placement of information,
and a color-coding system. A
typographic detail is provided
in the circle at right.

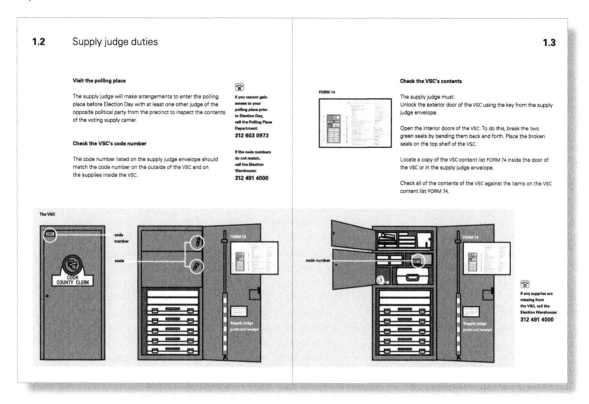

1.2 Supply judge duties

Visit the polling place

The supply judge will make arrangements to enter the polling place before Election Day with at least one other judge of the opposite political party from the precinct to inspect the contents of the voting supply carrier.

Check the VSC's code number

The code number listed on the supply judge envelope should match the code number on the outside of the VSC and on the supplies inside the VSC.

If you cannot gain access to your polling place prior to Election Day, call the Polling Place Department:
312 603 0973

If the code numbers do not match, call the Election Warehouse:
312 491 4000

1.3

Check the VSC's contents

FORM 74

The supply judge must:
Unlock the exterior door of the VSC using the key from the supply judge envelope.

Open the interior doors of the VSC. To do this, break the two green seals by bending them back and forth. Place the broken seals on the top shelf of the VSC.

Locate a copy of the VSC content list FORM 74 inside the door of the VSC or in the supply judge envelope.

Check all of the contents of the VSC against the items on the VSC content list FORM 74.

If any supplies are missing from the VSC, call the Election Warehouse:
312 491 4000

Above
These pages of the Cook County election judge manual demonstrate use of the Design for Democracy document management system.

Right
The Univers type was selected for its clarity, simplicity, and high degree of legibility. All components of the system use this single type family.

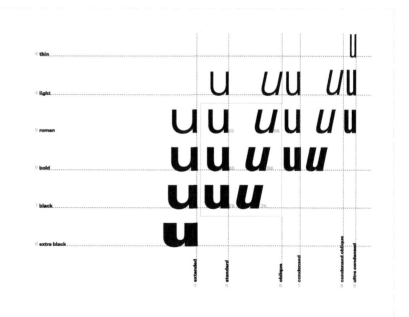

PROJECT:
O'Neil Identity

CLIENT:
O'Neil Printing

INTENDED AUDIENCE:
internal clients, print buyers
(designers, corporate print
buyers, corporations)

CREDITS:
copy, concept and design by
Rule29

↓

PRELIMINARY INVESTIGATION

O'Neil Printing, a service bureau with almost a century of experience, needed
to reconnect with its client base. It also needed to tailor its own internal
communications, enabling employees to project the O'Neil brand clearly to
an external audience. Rule29, a Chicago-based design firm, was engaged to
provide solutions. The Rule29 team conducted research to better understand
the client's personality,
unique service offerings,
and sales strategies.
Beginning with a literature
review and competitive
intelligence, designers
gathered information
about service bureaus of
similar size and scope.
"We looked at other
printers from their region

Rule29 built custom tools for assessing the effectiveness of the campaign.

and from around the country to see how like-minded companies talked about
themselves," says Rule29 principal Justin Ahrens. Through interviews conducted
with the O'Neil staff and customers, the designers were able to identify several
features that differentiated the company from other printers in the area. The
information collected in the preliminary research process provided Rule29 with a
solid foundation for design.

Application + Continued Assessment

Reinvigorating the O'Neil Printing brand called for a comprehensive redesign of
the company's marketing collateral. In addition to providing visual communication
services, Rule29 also built custom tools for assessing the effectiveness of the

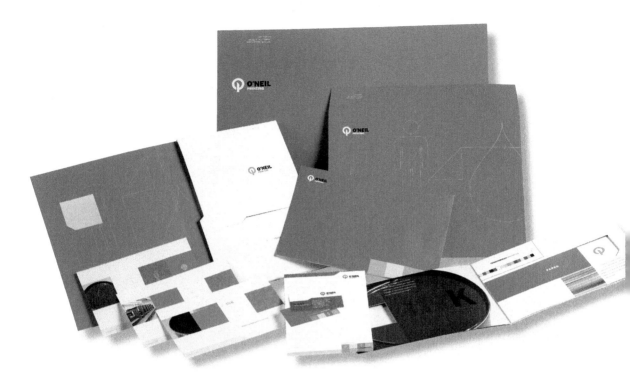

Above

Using research and consultation to identify target communication goals, Rule29 developed a graphic identity for O'Neil Printing. Applied in both print and electronic form (as shown in this image from their website), it has helped the 98-year-old service bureau increase business development and stand out in its community. Using proprietary software to assess the effectiveness of the campaign, Rule29 continues to update and adjust O'Neil's messaging.

Left

Research revealed that many print houses did not comprehensively market their individual identities. Rule29's solution to differentiate their client from its competitors was to extend the O'Neil brand across every surface, from traditional marketing materials (such as the media kit shown here) to less obvious choices such as building décor, press uniforms, job envelopes, delivery vehicles, and even email signatures.

campaign. By collecting key data from the O'Neil sales staff at regular intervals, and analyzing this information with customized spreadsheets, the design team could fine-tune the strategic messaging.

This ongoing iterative design process is mutually beneficial. It ensures that the client's material consistently meets market demands, and it engages Rule29 as a business consultant and strategic partner rather than a vendor retained on a project-by-project basis.

Below
Rule 29 discovered that O'Neil Printing had core capabilities, not all of which were immediately apparent to their customers. The designers used these marketable traits to create a series of four icons, identifying integral aspects of O'Neil's business. Shown here in an advertisement—Ink, Paper, People, Craft—are not only components of the printer's daily function but also a part of its philanthropic mission.

PROJECT:	CLIENT:	INTENDED AUDIENCE:	CREDITS:
Carnegie Library of Pittsburgh Branch Renovation Signage and Wayfinding	Carnegie Library of Pittsburgh	Pittsburgh public library users	Concept and design, Landesberg Design, with research assistance from MAYA Design, Inc.

A NEW CHAPTER

Landesberg Design was commissioned by the Carnegie Library of Pittsburgh (CLP) to develop an environment that was more accessible and functional for a broad range of branch users. The design had to reinforce the library's new identity and garner attention for improvements in collections, facilities, and services through renovations in signage and wayfinding.

Meeting Complex Needs

Because a wide range of individuals use the library for a number of different reasons, Landesberg was charged with creating visual communication tools that met the needs of all patrons. To accomplish their mission, Landesberg worked with MAYA Design, an award-winning information

"Research has the potential to affect our business practices significantly..."

architecture consultancy that was also hired by CLP. They applied a multilateral research approach by using several different qualitative tactics including role playing/performance research, ethnographic research, user surveys, user testing, and observation. Qualitative research, focused on understanding the "qualities" surrounding a specific subject, is often used to understand social human behavior that is not so easily described with statistical analysis. In this case, the design team set out to understand the user experience of library patrons.

Landesberg and MAYA didn't stop there. They conducted affinity diagramming, an organizational technique that helped to arrange library features into user-centered clusters. They also photographed and analyzed existing conditions at eighteen sites, engaging in lexicon and legibility studies. This collection of terms (such as "ask a librarian," "customer services," "discover more," etc.) determined a shared language of library patrons. They then prototyped signage solutions by hanging foam-core models in a variety of places—testing color, contrast, sight lines, distances, font styles, and sizes for appropriateness and legibility.

A Guiding Force

"Research was critical to establishing a language (both verbal and visual) for the system of signs," says Vicki Crowley of Landesberg. "Throughout the design process we checked concepts and solutions against data collected during the research phase." This careful attention to highlighted visibility considerations such as contrast, clarity of message, and font legibility would help build a dynamic and highly functional wayfinding system.

During their research, Landesberg used all the resources recommended by the Society for Environmental Graphic Design, and took advantage of SEGDTalk, an online forum for environmental graphic design professionals. The forum provided best practices information regarding type heights for maximum legibility at various distances, ADA (Americans with Disabilities Act) guidelines, as well as practical information about fabricators and materials.[26] Landesberg also researched other library systems and educational institutions that had recently undergone transformations, assessing the successes and failures of those projects.

An Ongoing Process

Landesberg received the results of an assessment conducted by MAYA following the grand opening of the Main branch (at which a dynamic signage system was designed and implemented by EDGE, the architecture firm commissioned to remodel the first floor of the Oakland institution). Much of the feedback centered on type size, sight lines, and scale—all legibility issues. Landesberg's design team then incorporated these recommendations, where appropriate for neighborhood locations, in their subsequent work on branch signage.

Landesberg recognizes the value of research in both its business relationships and project outcomes. "Research has the potential to affect our business practices significantly as clients become increasingly interested in quantifiable outcomes," says founder Rick Landesberg. "We see this interest as a good thing—hopefully, it will contribute to a more universal understanding of the significant contribution good design can make. In terms of our creative practices, additional research often improves our ability to focus on target audiences more effectively—strengthening the impact of our design work."

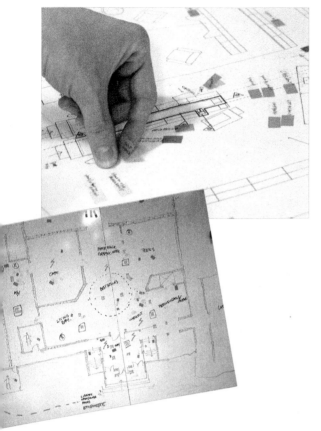

Left, Above
Using visualization and brainstorming focused on floor plans, the Landesberg team was able to create a patron-centered wayfinding system for library branches.

Below
Bright colors were used to create a focus on the library's logo, reinforcing CLP's commitment to the community in graphic form on the exterior of the building. The placement and size of the logo also provide passersby with a reminder of the library's location, on the second floor of the building. Says Rick Landesberg, "It announces—okay it screams— 'The library is up here!'"

Above
The signage developed for CLP is the result of numerous investigations into linguistic, aesthetic, and structural considerations.

Left

In their initial research, the design team explored library branches, capturing numerous examples of the graphic language of the institution. These photos show inconsistencies with the library's old signage.

Below

Playful typographic treatments were placed in the entranceway to reinforce the atmosphere of an approachable learning environment. Quotes from Pittsburgh authors were included to build local pride.

PROJECT:	CLIENT:	INTENDED AUDIENCE:	CREDITS:
A Drawing Manual by Thomas Eakins	Philadelphia Museum of Art, in a joint effort with the Pennsylvania Academy	students, scholars, curators, and individuals interested in American art and art education	Design, Baseman Design Associates

↓

HISTORY LESSON

When Frank Baseman of Baseman Design Associates got the opportunity to design and produce a historic volume, he dived in to the nineteenth-century research the project demanded. In Baseman's case, looking back in time allowed him to create the best design possible for a modern book. Baseman's historic research offers a fascinating look at a different approach to a set of design challenges.

Staying True to the Period

The Philadelphia Museum of Art and the Pennsylvania Academy enlisted Baseman to help publish a book entitled *A Drawing Manual by Thomas Eakins*. Because Eakins began writing the book roughly between 1881 and 1885, the design of the book needed to reflect both the time frame and the content accurately. Adding to the challenge, Eakin's book had never been published but was full of useful tips, diagrams, drawings, and suggestions for advanced study to accompany his text.

> # Baseman's historic research offers a fascinating look at a different approach to a set of design challenges.

Baseman's design needed to unite the original manuscript and the original drawings—together for the first time—in as true a manner as possible to the author's original intent.

Right
*Primary research conducted
at the American Philosophical
Society library in Philadelphia
gave insight into period
publications. Baseman studied
typeface selections, typographic
treatments, publication size,
printing techniques, and use of
imagery to design the Eakins
book accurately.*

A DRAWING MANUAL

BY

THOMAS EAKINS

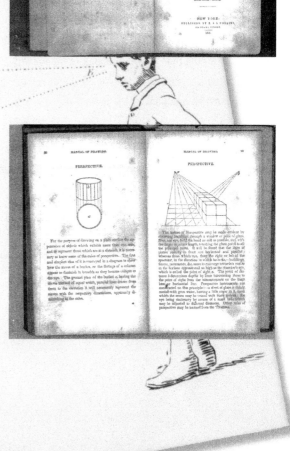

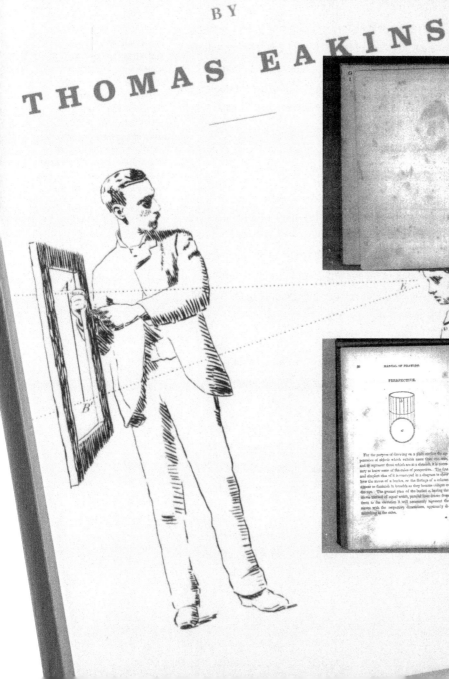

Learning the Language

"It was clear to me that I needed to investigate and conduct research as to what other publications would have looked like during that time," says Baseman. "The requirement was to design and produce the book faithfully, so that it was at least a nod to what might have been published had it been published in the first place."

Baseman began his research into typographic history by examining books, drawing manuals, and other documents published during the mid- to late nineteenth-century. Baseman conducted his primary research at the American Philosophical Society library in Philadelphia. He found multiple editions/printings of Rembrandt Peale's *Graphics: A Manual of Drawing and Writing for the Use of Schools and Families*, circa 1835–1850. He made photocopies of Peale's book, as well as other publications from this time period, to study the typeface selections, typographic treatments, size of publications, printing techniques, use of imagery, and other elements.

A Font of Knowledge

Baseman consulted with type designer and typographic historian Jonathan Hoefler, whose help and advice proved invaluable. Sending Hoefler sample pages from his literature review, Baseman requested guidance regarding typographic selections appropriate for the time period. Baseman's preliminary research, coupled with Hoefler's expertise, helped determine which fonts were realistic options: historically accurate but also practical for the project.

Solutions Rooted in History

In the end, Baseman's research allowed him to select a group of fonts that effectively conveyed the historic atmosphere of the project while remaining user-friendly to modern eyes.

"The design decisions I made in my contemporary practice were deeply influenced by the sense of typographic and graphic design history I encountered through the mid- to late nineteenth-century typographic examples I uncovered while conducting the research for this project," Baseman said. "And, ultimately, this related to the overall design of the book as well."

This book, the end product of Baseman's research, showcases the timeless elegance of Eakins' work while making its lessons clear to readers and staying true to its original era.

Opposite
In an effort to stay true to the period in which the Eakins book was written, all of Baseman's design decisions were driven by his research into design and typographic history. Baseman says he made aesthetic decisions based on what might have been appropriate when the book was first written, and also "as a contemporary designer, wanted to use well-designed, classic typefaces that have stood the test of time." The text was set in Century and Century Expanded (created in 1900), and display headings were set in Akzidenz-Grotesk and Clarendon (Clarendon created in 1845).[27] Illustrations were Eakins' own.

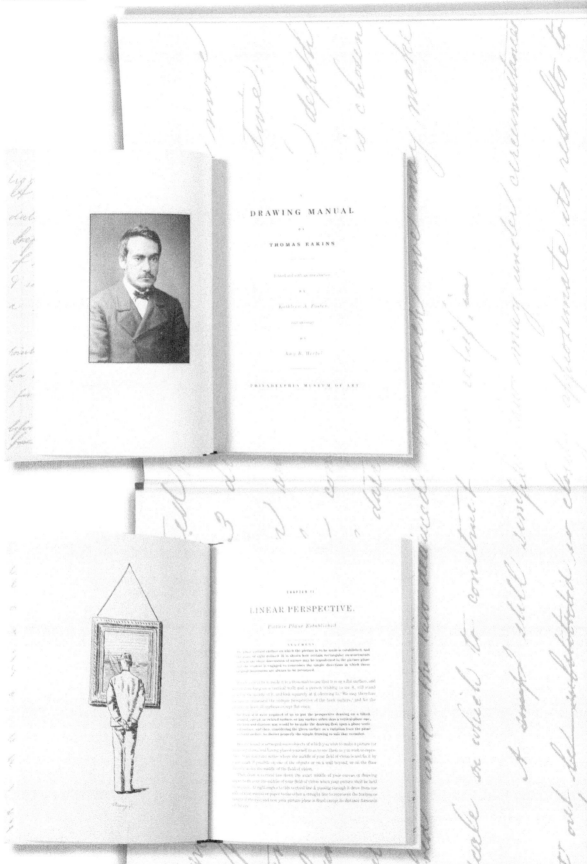

PROJECT:
Type 1 Tools

CLIENT:
Type 1 Tools

INTENDED AUDIENCE:
families and caregivers of children
with Type 1 diabetes

CREDITS:
Designers: Lisa Powell +
Doug Powell

KNOWLEDGE IS POWER

When designers Lisa and Doug Powell learned their daughter suffered from
Type 1 "juvenile onset" diabetes, design was the last thing on their minds. Instead,
they sought to learn all they could about the illness and the treatment options
for their child. The experience was bewildering and draining. Already shocked and
overwhelmed by the diagnosis of a serious disease, they were disheartened to
find a dearth of quality
educational materials for
families affected by
the illness.

The designers became
voracious researchers,
endeavoring to learn all
the complex information
needed to give the
best care and ensure
the best treatment

"We were not only designers but entrepreneurs and product developers."

for their child. This was particularly trying in the midst of a traumatic emotional
crisis, especially because the health of their child depended on a strict regimen of
mealtime calculations and insulin delivery. The designers recognized a clear design
opportunity because the educational products available to parents were clinical,
technical, intimidating, and completely un-kid-friendly.

An Effective Prescription

The designers created a successful set of tools by working closely with a network of
diabetes professionals and families living with the disease. Their research relied on
the experts and families to provide feedback and guidance and to review prototypes.
"We were constantly researching and testing our ideas as we developed the design

Above, Right
Handy "FlashCarbs" provide a fun
and simple way to deliver vital
nutritional information to children
with Type 1 diabetes.

for these products," Doug Powell says. "In this case we were not only designers but entrepreneurs and product developers."

The result of their efforts was Type 1 Tools, a set of products that provides facts about the disease, as well as information on treatment and nutrition, all in an easy-to-use package. Type 1 Tools provides clear, concise, and critical information on Type 1 diabetes in an effective, empowering, and kid-friendly way.

Resarch Proves Key

Research proved that the target demographic for this project is typically Web-savvy, so Type 1 Tools are available for sale online. They also learned that health-care privacy regulations prevent direct contact with the customer (at least until the customer establishes it). Therefore, the Powells had to consider and plan carefully what kinds of collateral to create and then think about how to get it in the hands of children and families in need. Ultimately, the Type 1 Tools comprehensive website became the best vehicle for information and products, because viewers could use the site in the privacy of their homes or even access it with their doctor during an office visit. The Powells leaned on connections they had made while researching in the medical and diabetic communities to spread the word about their project and direct traffic to their site. At that point the partnership of research and design proved its merit, as the consumer market eagerly received the Type 1 Tools product line.

Solving an unframed problem proved to be transformative for the Powells. As they continue to fine-tune their research process, the designers recognize its value in multiple stages of development. "We find that, generally speaking, the more seriously we take the research aspect, the more smoothly the creative process goes," Doug Powell says. Not only do they bill for research, they also have learned to be insistent with clients, emphasizing the need to include time and budget for research.

A Rewarding Achievement

The Powells' passionate and dedicated research on Type 1 Tools helped create a well-designed resource, rewarding on several levels. Not only were the designers able to help families and children in need, they also boosted their own knowledge and learned how to better care for their daughter. There was also a surprise benefit: "Interestingly," Doug Powell says, "our new expertise as diabetes industry insiders with a design/communication specialty has garnered us several new consulting clients."

type1tools ™

Hot Dog
W/ BUN & KETCHUP

Rice
1/2 CUP COOKED

Peas
1/2 CUP COOKED

12g

Fish
ALL KINDS
NOT BATTERED

0g

© 2003 TYPE 1 TOOLS LLC

Top
Type 1 Tools is all about accessibility. The animated logo sets the tone for an approachable, user-friendly set of tools for people of all ages.

Bottom
Vibrant magnets carry critical nutrition statistics. Visually appealing, they are easily mounted in many areas around the kitchen, reinforcing the good eating habits vital to children with Type 1 diabetes.

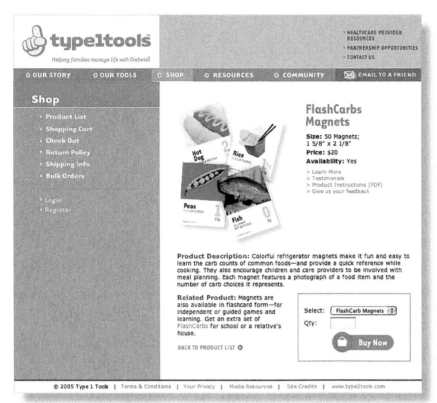

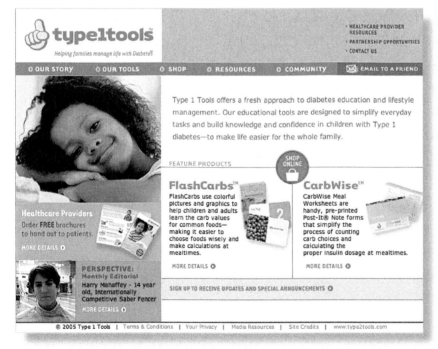

PROJECT:	CLIENT:	INTENDED AUDIENCE:	CREDITS:
Ace Rebranding and Marketing Materials	Ace Express Pallets	manufacturing, distribution, and wholesale companies that require a fast, efficient overnight distribution service within the thirty-two counties of Ireland	Dara Creative

↓

NEW BUSINESS, NEW OPPORTUNITY

Dara Creative of Dublin, Ireland, had to rebrand and build a marketing program for Ace Express Pallets, an overnight nationwide distribution service. This service was the first of its kind in Ireland, so the branding and collateral had to identify Ace Express Pallets as an innovative market leader. The branding had to be visible day and night on the road, inspire confidence in customers, and reflect the shared values of all twelve network-member organizations.

To support the new brand identity, Dara created marketing materials including transportation carrier graphics, a corporate brochure, information packs, promotional maps, company stationery, and a website with online tracking.

"Rather than designing for the sake of it, we have become more calculated in our approach."

Research Sharpens Focus

Dara Creative relied on market research, competitive intelligence, and user testing to define its strategy and create a successful campaign. "Our market research indicated that this is an industry dominated by men," said Marigold Freeman of Dara Creative. "This strongly influenced the design style, which consists of a bold, unfussy brand in masculine shades of blue and silver. Our research suggests that this modern and approachable style is also appealing to women." But communicating

Opposite: Left
The development of a mood board set the visual tone for the Ace identity and subsequent design collateral.

with the target audience was only part of the challenge, they also needed to stand out from their competitors.

Opposite: Right
Dara Creative thoroughly documented its visualization exercises, creating this workbook that showcases the graphic development of the Ace brand.

Dara Creative prides itself on its ability to differentiate its clients from their competitors. Hence, competitive research is crucial to their work. Although Ace Express Pallets had no direct competitors in Ireland, Dara researched similar companies in the U.K., other freight companies, and companies in related industries so they could develop a distinct brand that would not get lost in a sea of sameness.

For Ace Express Pallets vehicles, practical concerns such as nighttime visibility and discoloration of materials were considered. After initially selecting yellow for the logo, research indicated that such a color often fades and can be difficult to clean and repair. Silver was selected as a replacement.

One Design, Multiple Messages

From the beginning, Dara Creative used the information gathered during research to give shape to its design. As a logistics firm, the client needed a strong, modern image that was clean and crisp but also conveyed a message of speed and efficiency. The creative team referenced design magazines, company brochures, and other literature to develop a functional approach.

In the early stages of the design process, Dara Creative compared its sketches to numerous relevant industry logos. The simplicity of Dara's design made it stand out from the rest. They used a similar process to inform the aesthetic of the website, referencing screen captures of competitors' websites so the client could make comparisons.

Dara Creative's research indicated that a strong, visual road presence was crucial to the project, which ultimately translated into a modern, clean brand that suggested the client's key deliverables of speed and reliability. This bold, masculine design was carried through the Ace website, info packages, promotional maps, and stationery system, creating collateral that is straightforward, accessible, and consistent. Communication benchmarks of strength, clarity, practicality, and visual presence—delineated by their research—provided a focus for the design, creating a mark that would appeal to a wide range of clients and prospects.

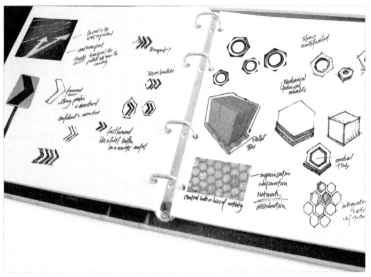

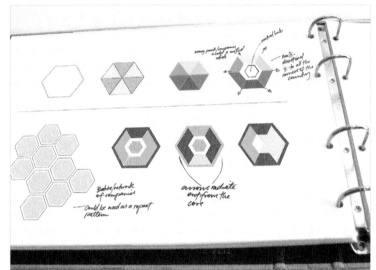

Right

In a rebrand of Ace Express Pallets, Dara Creative's market research found that the color palette of blue and silver appealed not only to their client's male-dominated target audience but to women as well. Further research into the color palette found that silver was a strong choice for practical reasons: it's easier to clean and service, with less fading over time.

Researching for Success

For Dara Creative, the research process helps ensure creative success. Rather than start with a blank slate and no support, it outlines key communication requirements. "Rather than designing for the sake of it, we have become more calculated in our approach," Freeman said. The process has created financial dividends as well. "Research has made us more focused in our work," Freeman continues. "This means that our work is less wasteful and our message is clear at a much earlier stage. This saves time for both designer and client, leading to cost savings for both parties."

Opposite
It was important that the new Ace identity, as applied to a fleet of vehicles, was easily recognizable both during the day and in low light situations.

Left, Above
Communication benchmarks of strength, clarity, and practicality provided a thematic focus for design collateral such as this stationery system and map of Ireland.

PROJECT:
World Trade Centers
Association global positioning
and branding update

CLIENT:
World Trade Centers Association

INTENDED AUDIENCE:
primary, local WTC leadership;
secondary, international business/
world trade community

CREDITS:
creative director, Christopher
Liechty; art director, Jeff Johnson;
designers, Hiedi Blackwelder, Nick
Redd, David Dick, Jane Clayson

DEFINING A BRAND

The World Trade Centers Association (WTCA) called on Meyer & Liechty, Inc., an
American firm specializing in cross-cultural design, to revitalize their brand. The
designers set to work, building a strategy to refocus messaging and bring greater
consistency to WTCA communications. The goal was clear, but achieving it required
considerable research and creative development, particularly because of the unique
nature of the WTCA.

The international business
climate at the time of
this brand revitalization
project was changing
dramatically. Thus, it
was clear that refocusing
the WTCA's message
to emphasize the
association's network of
more than 275 entities in

Great research doesn't have to be expensive or complicated.

cities around the world would be fundamental to its success.

The Power of Listening

Meyer & Liechty began by undertaking a brand audit to review existing WTCA
materials and learn about the visual history of the organization. They focused
primarily on ethnographic research, conducting interviews with leaders and staff
members of several World Trade Centers, as well as members of the international
business community. "We also had an unusual opportunity to attend an event held
by the AIGA New York Chapter and *Metropolis* magazine to discuss the future naming
of the World Trade Center site," said Christopher Liechty.

WORLD TRADE CENTERS ASSOCIATION

Above, Right
Previously there was no unified identity program for the World Trade Centers Association. Meyer & Liechty developed a comprehensive system of collateral that could be used by any Center, regardless of location. Through their research, the firm discovered common messaging that would promote the shared values of all WTCs, such as the phrase shown on these materials: "Peace and stability through trade."

Top
The new World Trade Centers Association logo focuses the core of the identity on the global network of 275 WTCs and the business service that they provide: promoting world trade.

The results of that event surprised Liechty. "It was very interesting to learn that despite the fame of the New York World Trade Center, the World Trade Centers Association was virtually unknown," he said. "It was also interesting to observe that people believed that no 'world trade' activities were happening in the center despite the fact that every tenant in the New York buildings was required by law to be involved in world trade activities."

Old-Fashioned Legwork

Great research doesn't have to be expensive or complicated. Because Liechty is involved in many international business events in the normal course of his business, opportunities were plentiful, and he was able to carry out most of the research with no budget. When traveling to a city with a WTC, Liechty was sure to visit that Center and interview employees. He also attended WTC global meetings and interviewed WTC leadership from various cities around the world, seizing every opportunity to interview members of the business community, including international business students.

New Needs Identified

These extensive interviews paid off when it became clear that the strongest value offered by the World Trade Centers Association was access to local WTC leadership with extensive contacts in local markets.

The WTCA had historically focused on property development and providing building space for businesses involved in world trade. Professional services, now identified as holding key value, were offered later in the development of the organization by only some WTCs. This explains why the service or network message was not a focus of previous branding efforts.

A Theme Emerges

Research helped Meyer & Liechty create a hierarchy of messages that would then be applied to collateral across the campaign. "WTCA is a global network of World Trade Centers" was the primary message. "Peace and Stability through Trade" was established as a singular tagline. Though the organization had already used these and many other statements, Meyer & Liechty helped the WTCA focus all efforts on these two declarations to create clear communication across international borders.

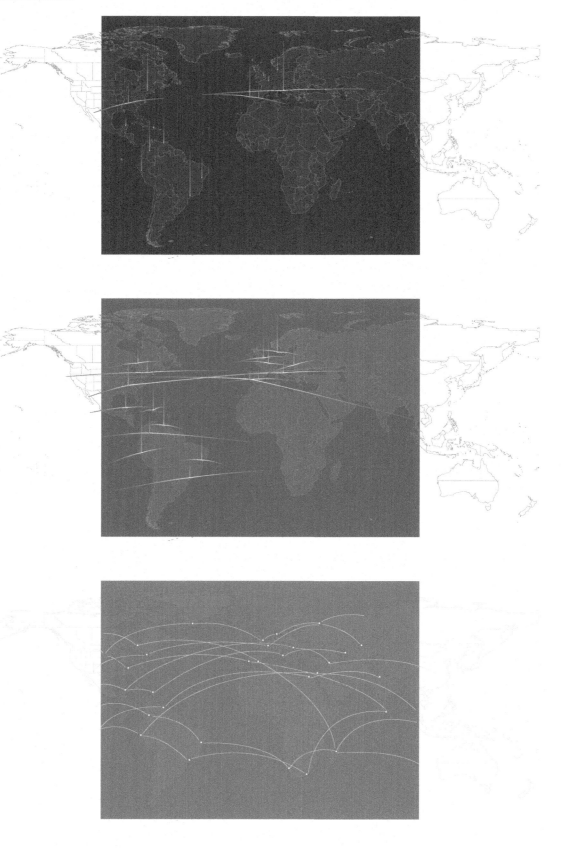

A Clear Vision

After selecting their primary message, Meyer & Liechty sought to communicate it through both words and visuals. The graphic image used at the bottom of most materials imbues a spirit of the WTCA global network. This image became more descriptive as animated points of light (cities) on a world map morphed into a connective grid. The photos of various WTCs, presented in a woven pattern, also reinforce this message.

Hitting the Bullseye

Using research, Meyer & Liechty discovered that the concept of a global network was of primary value and interest to the international business community. That theme was then applied to collateral, focusing on the WTCA network of services and the social impact of world trade. Meyer and Liechty gained conceptual buy-in from their client by framing concepts with research and by documenting their investigations. The design team provided the client with multiple interview reports throughout the initial research phase, which fostered a sense of cooperation and agreement between designer and client regarding project requirements. This collaboration with the client proved invaluable, resulting in a comprehensive communications project for a large, culturally diverse, and decentralized organization.

PROJECT:	CLIENT:	INTENDED AUDIENCE:	CREDITS:
Vitacress Salads Packaging Design	Vitacress	consumers of salad greens in Portugal	Design Firm: Financial Designs; designer, Ludwig Haskins

↓

DESIGN IS EVERYTHING

When Vitacress Salads, a British supplier of salad and specialty vegetables, launched a line of washed, bagged baby leaf lettuce in the new market of Portugal, it faced numerous challenges. Beyond entrenched competition, Vitacress had no brand presence in Portugal and chose not to advertise for the launch. In short, the package appearing on market shelves would be consumers' first introduction to both the company and its products, so the design had to stand out while making a statement of upscale sophistication. Vitacress called on Financial Designs, a London firm with whom they had previously worked, to undertake this critical project.

The product went from being unknown to garnering a 33% market share within twenty months.

Goals

Vitacress had three goals.

First was the launch of Vitacress as a premium consumer brand. Second was to use this launch to increase group sales, which would make better use of its Iberian growing capacity. Finally, Vitacress wanted closer control over marketing and packaging of its own products. Turning Vitacress into a consumer brand would overcome the company's previous reliance on other brands to sell its wares; lack of control over how its products were presented and sold had become a major frustration.

Susana Pais, Vitacress' product manager in Portugal, was responsible for the development of this new initiative. "When we embarked on the project we knew an excellent packaging design would make all the difference," she said. "When consumers approach the point of sale, only 20 percent know exactly what they are going to buy; the other 80 percent need a little help. Innovation and breakthrough were essential if we were to differentiate our product as a premium brand."

A Lifetime of Research

Ludwig not only brought his years as a designer to the project, he also had the advantage of having worked with Vitacress on a number of previous projects, so he had a keen understanding of the company's culture and needs. Additionally, Haskins is passionate and knowledgeable about agriculture, having spent many childhood holidays on his grandfather's farm in South Africa. Pais notes, "His experience and insight into the challenges we face were a major advantage."

With no budget for consumer research or focus groups, Haskins had to rely on his own design expertise and personal judgment, so he researched supermarket shelves to gauge how other brands communicate premium quality through design and how products appear in the store environment.

The Clear Solution to Clear Bags

"All other bagged salads came in clear bags carrying hard-to-read type; we decided that in an aisle of green produce a white background should be used to provide a fresh, clean canvas for text and illustration," Haskins says. "This would sit in the upper half of the bag—allowing the consumer to see some of what was inside while covering the empty space above the salad."

Haskins chose to use illustrations to compliment the design. "If a photograph of a raw product is shown next to an actual raw product, there will always be a mismatch between the two," says Haskins. "The relatively strong differences in leaf outline for the different varieties of salad used in the bag provided clear inspiration for an illustration that would become a simple icon to differentiate it from rival products on the shelf."

From looking at store shelves and using his past experience, Haskins decided on a matte varnish for the opaque areas of the packaging to make typography more legible and add a premium, silky feel to the bags. "It's an idea I borrowed from premium crisps packaging and various drinks," Haskins explains. "Full gloss packaging under bright florescent supermarket lighting leads to a sea of shiny packs that look like cheap sweets."

A Measurable Triumph

Sales exceeded twelve-month forecasts by more than 40 percent, and Vitacress captured more than 40 percent of the supermarket display space available for like products. By challenging the category's design conventions, the product went from being unknown to garnering a 33 percent market share within twenty months of launch.

Opposite: Top
Vitacress credits the package design of their ready-to-eat salads for exceeding sales forecasts by 40 percent, capturing 40 percent of supermarket display space, and capturing 33 percent market share in twenty months!

Opposite: Bottom
Traditional approaches to washed and ready-to-eat salads result in a "sea of green," causing brand confusion while camouflaging the product inside. Financial Designs' approach made the Vitacress choice very clear.

Vitacress is now a nationally recognized brand sold in more than 200 Portuguese supermarkets, and the Portuguese division's total gross sales are up more than 60 percent. As an added benefit, when the scale of production stepped up with increased sales, unit production costs fell.

The success of Vitacress Baby Leaf Salad has also created sixty jobs in the Alentejo agricultural region where Vitacress built its new factory. Vitacress is now moving ahead with plans to roll out the product in Spain and the U.K. They credit most of the success to the packaging.[28]

This Page
Among the many design decisions surrounding the Vitacress packaging, Haskins paid special attention to the color and finish of the bags to showcase the contents. Using illustrations instead of a more common photographic approach further differentiates the Vitacress products on supermarket shelves.

PROJECT:	CLIENT:	INTENDED AUDIENCE:	CREDITS:
Rebranding for Dublin Chamber of Commerce	Dublin Chamber of Commerce	members and potential members	Dara Creative

ONE BANNER, MANY FACES

In order for Dara Creative to build a new brand for the Dublin Chamber of Commerce, it needed to reflect the chamber's extremely diverse membership and project an image of a vibrant, progressive, and dynamic organization. To accomplish this, Dara Creative relied on several forms of research.

Uncovering Existing Problems

By reviewing existing Dublin Chamber print materials, Dara Creative found inconsistencies in logo usage that were adversely affecting the visibility and image of the organization. This helped strengthen the case for a new logo with clearly defined

"**Our research was invaluable in more clearly identifying the client's needs.**"

parameters for its use. Combining a literature review with competitor analysis laid the foundation for a focused approach.

A Helping Hand

For this project Dara Creative worked with a marketing research company (Brand Dynamics) who sent questionnaires to staff and members of Dublin Chamber of Commerce to identify issues with the existing brand and pinpoint values that the new brand identity should convey. What they learned was that chamber members saw the organization as a trustworthy business leader that provides valuable lobbying and networking services. Moreover, those surveyed suggested a modern brand reflecting the Dublin Chamber's progressive status.

In response to this input, the design team began building an uncluttered logo that emphasized Dublin, its culture, and its history.

Shaping a Solution

Dara Creative then used Web-based research of other chambers of commerce throughout the world to analyze the quality of their branding in comparison with that of the Dublin Chamber. This gave the designers solid background knowledge of the market, and identified how the Dublin Chamber was positioned.

A Compelling Direction

"Our research was invaluable in more clearly identifying the client's needs," said Brian Maher of Dara Creative. "The client wanted to portray the chamber's valuable commercial history but also its vibrancy in the present and future. It wanted to be seen as a progressive and influential communicator, providing invaluable networking and lobbying services."

The new brand identity reflects the city and the rich traditions of the Dublin Chamber and its members. The brand features a castle, a spire, and a bridge. The castle, which is situated in the heart of south Dublin city, was chosen as a representation of the chamber's wealth of knowledge and experience. The spire sits in the north city and represents future progression—the key need for the new logo as identified by research findings. The bridge is the uniting element, capturing the networking aspect of the Dublin Chamber.

The initial research was a very influential factor in the success of the final mark. "The survey results indicated that the focus of the new brand should be on Dublin—and hence provided a valuable starting point for the designer," said Maher. "The brand values indicated that the final brand should be youthful and energetic—traits which are incorporated in the finished product."

Right

Dara Creative used surveys to better understand the client's needs and to inform their redesign for the Dublin Chamber of Commerce. The new identity reflects the traditions of the organization while promoting an energetic and forward-thinking approach. The castle, situated in the heart of south Dublin city, symbolizes the Chamber's wealth of knowledge and experience. The spire, situated in the north, represents the future. The bridge captures the networking focus of the group.

Below

Research indicated that Dara should place the focus of the brand on the city of Dublin while reflecting a fresh, youthful outlook. Summative review, conducted in the form of a client satisfaction survey, reinforced the success of the project.

dublinchamber
of commerce

PROJECT:
HOW magazine Redesign

CLIENT:
F&W Publications and *HOW* magazine

INTENDED AUDIENCE:
designers

CREDITS:
a collaborative project between *HOW* in-house designer Tricia Bateman, the *HOW* editorial staff, and design by DJ Stout and Erin Mayes, Pentagram Design, Austin, Texas

↓

A VERY TOUGH CROWD

Maintaining a fresh look is critical for *HOW* magazine, a publication aimed squarely at graphic designers. So when the staff decided it was time for a redesign, they had to develop a plan that would lead to both a creative and a practical solution. They quickly realized this sizable undertaking required research that would provide a comprehensive look at the magazine, its brand, and its audience.

A Two-Pronged Attack

Because *HOW*'s staff knows their audience and mission so intimately, they could execute the redesign in house. However, for the sake of time, perspective, and publicity, they concluded

Pentagram used in-depth research to frame the project.

it would be ideal to hire an outside firm to undertake the actual redesign. DJ Stout of Pentagram Design, a designer with a good deal of magazine design experience, and a firm that is well respected and recognized by their design constituency, was the clear choice for the job.

Charting a Course

In preparation for the redesign, *HOW* conducted reader surveys, collected market information, and requested specific feedback from their advisory board, Friends of *HOW*, which cumulatively gave them a strong definition of their brand. The advisory board, which is a highly effective way to monitor one's company or organization, consists of a diverse group with an interest in the magazine. These "friends" range from practicing designers to industry superstars, all of whom provide insightful, honest, and invaluable feedback.

Above
Pentagram increased the size of
HOW's masthead and rendered it
in a way that links it thematically
with the focus of each issue.

The magazine's staff provided Stout with all of their findings, collected samples of effective editorial design, and compiled a thorough list of questions about defining the magazine's brand and challenges regarding the *HOW* staff's use of the old design. With that information, Stout had an accurate understanding of their brand, their vision, and the audience to which they cater.

Pentagram and *HOW* staffers worked together to define five overarching goals for the redesign:

- *Enhance the service aspect.* HOW *is a reader benefit-oriented magazine, and that should be enhanced, not lost, in the redesign.*

- *Give it personality.* HOW's *brand is that of an approachable friend and the redesign should reflect that.*

- *Keep the design flexible.* *The redesign has to accommodate a small staff and budget with wide-ranging visuals.*

- *Celebrate the lifestyle.* *Designers are passionate about their work, and the redesign should reflect that excitement.*

- *Generate excitement.* *The redesign should attract new readers, new advertisers, and as much publicity as possible.*

Advice from "Friends"

As they had hoped, the Friends of *HOW* provided important feedback, which confirmed much of their initial research but also outlined exactly what its readers wanted. Because the research came directly from its passionate readers, *HOW* could be confident about the accuracy of the input. "We found out that readers like to look at work samples as much as they like to read about them," said Bateman, who led the project. "Therefore, word counts could go down, and images could get bigger. Pertinent information could be redirected into captions. We found out that readers liked the personality we projected and thought it was as important as the content. Therefore, we kept our more conceptual content and steered away from a minimalist or stark design."

The Execution

Pentagram used *HOW*'s in-depth research to frame the project, but infused the design with an individuality that sets the magazine apart from all its competitors. "We came up with a cover direction that demonstrated creative collaboration," said designer DJ Stout of Pentagram. Responsive to circulation statistics that illustrated *HOW*'s dominance on the newsstand, the designers determined not to make any sweeping changes to the masthead. Instead they leveraged the opportunity to allow other creatives to reinterpret the mark, creating a logo that is sometimes photographic, sometimes illustrative, but always rendered to reflect the content of each issue with their distinctive, attenuated capital letters.

Opposite: Top
Pentagram suggested using Parisine by Porchez Typofounderie for headline copy because of its unique personality and legibility. More design flexibility was achieved by changing the column structure of interior pages.

Opposite: Bottom
Pentagram initially presented the HOW staff with five concepts for the cover design, which they narrowed down to two. The covers are shown here in spreads from a HOW article reviewing the process.

THE CONCEPT With this typographically driven solution, Pentagram proposed that each issue's features would be presented as a series of "how to" sentences—a mini table of contents on the cover.

THE VERDICT This idea was rejected because tailoring cover lines to fit this layout configuration would have been restrictive and time-consuming.

THE CONCEPT Reminiscent of the blue-lined paste-up boards that were used before computers, this direction represented design work in progress and supported HOW's instructional focus.

THE VERDICT Although HOW's staff was intrigued by its retro nature, they were concerned that the concept's link with print design might alienate interactive designers. The outlined logo's reduced visibility was also a problem.

THE CONCEPT Pentagram rendered HOW's logo in a way that thematically links with the focus of each issue. The cover would feature a photograph of a designer at work, connecting with HOW's audience in a friendly way.

THE VERDICT The team's favorite from the logo. They asked Pentagram to develop additional cover options using conceptual subjects for variety.

...W with five cover
...nt.

staff responded mos...

The body was retooled as well to make the magazine more reader friendly (plenty of room for visuals), and easier for the *HOW* staff to work with. They needed a flexible grid, as past iterations of page structure had been difficult to work with and were often broken, creating inconsistency. "The interior design is very informative—lots of captions, charts, and diagrams to relate visually the informative nature of the editorial content," says Stout, whose alteration of the magazine's grid structure provided room for these additional visuals.

Readers and staff alike have welcomed the new face of the magazine, largely because they were an integral part of the process. The magazine continues to be a leading design publication in the United States, largely because Pentagram's redesign incorporated what research uncovered during the planning process. Not only does the publication now present itself in a manner that more accurately reflects its content and brand, but readers are also able to enjoy the benefits of a magazine tailored to their interests and needs.

Below
Adding more white space to content spreads helps readers quickly delineate content from advertisements.

Opposite
Research indicated that the magazine's audience liked looking at examples of work as much as reading about them. The new format allows for maximizing the impact of both written and image-driven content because the grid system allows for flexibility from story to story.

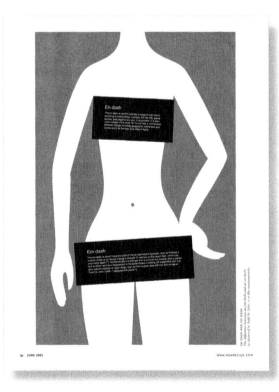

TRAVEL + CURIOSITY C CREATIVITY

FATE + FORTUNE N NEW YORK CITY

FIGURE 6.—BIG FLAT LOOP SPOKE

Text messaging has bred new generations of lazy typists, prompting many a die-hard grammarian to mourn the demise of the English language. Old-school conventions like punctuation, it seems, have become optional, if not passé. Are apostrophes and commas fading relics of written discourse, soon to go the way of the powdered wig and the quill pen? The semicolon may already be dead in the grave. And who the *#$@!% ever knew what a caret was for in the first place? Leave it to type devotees to brush the dust off and find out. That was David Schimmel's thought back in 2003. Schimmel, founder of New York City's And Partners, was searching for an antidote to what he calls the "dark era of bare-boned, utilitarian paper promotions" stemming from a weak economy and lingering fears over national security. If anyone could breathe new life into those arcane marks, designers could. And what better medium than old-fashioned paper?

---

glyphic tradition

PROJECT:	CLIENT:	INTENDED AUDIENCE:	CREDITS:
Killington Ski Resort Rebrand	American Skiing Company (ASC)	ASC corporate staff, Killington staff, East Coast skiers and Killington clientele	Sterling Brands, creative director, Marcus Hewitt; design directors, Stephanie Krompier, Dan Walter; planning directors, Jonathan Lee, Mike Bainbridge

STAYING ON TOP

American Skiing Company's (ASC) Killington ski resort had long been considered one of the East Coast's best skiing destinations, but the brand was losing its leading cachet. ASC brought in Sterling Brands to create an identity that captured the unique personality and essence of Killington while making it more relevant to today's skiers.

Sterling Brands first helped define the overall positioning and personality of Killington, then developed a new identity that would translate to all brand communications, including on-mountain signage, the website, advertising, and collateral.

"Research inspires and focuses our design practice."

Research Provides a Lift

Research formed the foundation for the entire project. A literature review included analysis of all competitive collateral, an examination of previous Killington client surveys, and a review of other research previously conducted by the client. Sterling then tested a range of positioning and preliminary visual themes in an online survey of 600 Killington and competitive resort skiers, representing a range of demographics. This targeted research helped Sterling understand how Killington was perceived and how it could once again be instantly identified as the premier ski resort on the East Coast.

The results gathered from the online survey provided both the strategic and aesthetic direction for the solution. These findings not only helped establish the athletic and contemporary tone of the project, but also pinpointed key communication tools for branding initiatives.

This Page

Sterling Brands has developed a proprietary research strategy called BEES, which they used to develop a comprehensive brand strategy for Killington Ski Resort. Using competitor analysis, focus groups, and interviews, Sterling refined not only the mark and communication materials, but also the strategic positioning of the resort. To the delight of the client, Sterling accomplished its goal of "creating an identity that captures and fuels the energy of the mountain."

By engaging their client as a partner in the research process, Sterling was able to illustrate the accuracy of the data collected. When they reached a design solution both parties recognized the concept that performed most effectively: the pride and thrill of "living large." The Killington resort is known for its fast and challenging runs, and the new mark was designed to capture that energy and dynamism. Commissioning a custom font and showcasing the mountain peak through a right to left tapered cut of blue, the design team conveyed the passion of the driving concept, which would motivate and connect with their established target audience.

Part of Every Solution

For Sterling, research plays a crucial role in every project, so much so that they use an in-house strategic planning team for that purpose on most projects. The Sterling system for research is called BEES (Brand Equity Evaluation System). This proprietary diagnostic and projective process measures visual brand equity and guides future brand design direction. The BEES process starts with comprehensive competitor analysis that informs visual explorations. These visuals are tested using surveys and focus groups that are scored based on participant feedback. The most successful solutions are then presented to the client along with a report that outlines the most effective means of implementation.

The commitment to research yields handsome dividends for Sterling. "Our research capability is often a determining factor in differentiating our business," says Sterling's Debbie Millman. "The ability of our practice to seamlessly integrate strategy, research, and design is a critical factor in our success and seen as a huge benefit to many clients."

Research often helps ensure a thoroughly satisfied client and a long-term successful relationship for Sterling. Not only does it lead to outstanding design direction, it also provides qualitative and/or quantitative evaluation of projects.

Millman notes, "Research inspires and focuses our design practice."

PROJECT:
The Art Institute of Chicago
website

CLIENT:
The Art Institute of Chicago

INTENDED AUDIENCE:
museum visitors, museum
members, educators, the
general public

CREDITS:
Studio Blue; Art Direction:
Cheryl Towler Weese and Kathy
Fredrickson; Design: Tammy Baird;
Information architecture: Matt
Simpson; Programming: Tiffany
Farriss and George D. Demet,
Palantir.net

ART FOR EVERYONE

After years of benignly neglecting its website, the Art Institute of Chicago contracted Studio Blue to develop a redesign that would accurately portray the museum as one of the world's finest. This initiative came about because of a change in museum leadership; therefore the timeline was compressed, and expectations were high.

Studio Blue sought to create a site that would communicate the diversity and uniqueness of the Art Institute of Chicago experience and convey the accessibility of the site and museum without sacrificing intelligence. In an effort to dispel the widely held belief that the museum was not family friendly, the designers needed to

The amount of time visitors spend on the site has increased enormously.

communicate that it was a destination point with many types of activities, including art appreciation. The site also needed to convey that there is always something new happening at the museum, of interest to everyone; while celebrating the richness of the museum's permanent collection, which includes many popular cultural icons.

Research Guides Mission

Although Studio Blue has a long relationship with the Institute, which helped them understand priorities and how to achieve consensus, they did a lot of research to bolster what they already knew about their client and its needs.

Studio Blue built a library of website examples that included major museums across the country, analyzed the strengths and weaknesses of those sites, then considered how to differentiate the AIC from the others to better represent a Midwestern museum with an internationally famous collection.

Studio Blue also did a series of small group interviews that helped more clearly define project requirements. Themes emerging from those interviews were: the museum was perceived as inaccessible to families; the other resources available to visitors, such as performances and children's activities, were not well known; and the museum's collections were not organized in a way that was easy for the general public to browse or reference online.

In addition to the research Studio Blue conducted, the museum had previously worked with a Web developer to do an evaluation of their website, including stakeholder interviews and in-depth comparisons of the site's content and structure with other museum sites. This additional perspective, though from an earlier point, helped the designers map the information architecture portion of the project.

Site Wins Fans

The research helped pinpoint key goals, which led to a design strategy that was a touchstone for the visual solution: the revolving art on the home page changes with repeat visits and uses simple interactive tools to engage the user. The word and image pairings evoke accessibility and convey the richness of the museum's collections, communicating that the museum is "a place for you," whoever you are. The user-friendly calendar can be searched by date, event, event type, museum program, or keyword.

Studio Blue is planning a detailed summative analysis of the site's effectiveness, but after just six months of use, the amount of time visitors spend on the site has increased enormously. The museum has also received a lot of mail (both digital and on paper) from happy users.

Opposite: Top
Using small group interviews, competitor analysis of other major art museums, and Web metric data, Studio Blue was able to convey the Midwestern family-friendly atmosphere of a museum with an international collection. This triangulation of research was critical to the successful redesign of the Institute's website. Online traffic has increased significantly.

Opposite: Bottom
By focusing on the needs of the user, Studio Blue developed friendly tools for the Institute's Calendar of Events, allowing the viewer to search by month, type of event, museum program, or keyword. Recognizing that each user has unique needs and interests, Studio Blue sought to create tools that would meet multiple demands.

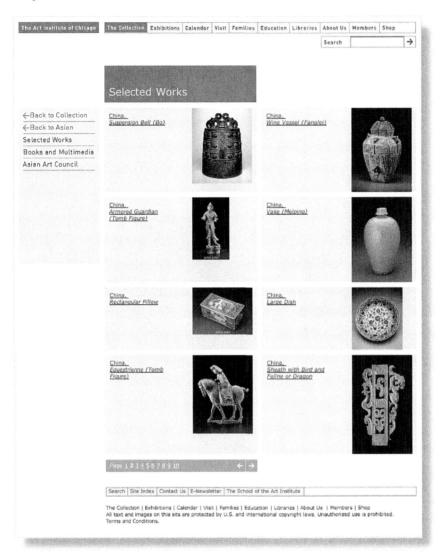

This Page

Studio Blue identified problems with the structure of content in the museum's website. Information was organized in a way that made sense to an audience with specialized knowledge of art and art history, but not to the general public. Studio Blue restructured the information, tailoring access to the needs of a broader audience.

The museum's galleries were reorganized on the new site to be accessible for any user—from professors to elementary school students.

PROJECT:	**CLIENT:**	**INTENDED AUDIENCE:**	**CREDITS:**
A Guide to Georgetown Law Center	Georgetown Law Center	accepted students who have not yet made the decision whether to attend	KINETIK, Inc.; Design: Jeff Fabian, Sam Shelton, Beth Clawson, Beverley Hunter, Jenny Skillman, Brad Ireland, Jackie Ratsch, Scott Rier; Photography: Mark Finkenstaedt, Washington, D.C.

INSPIRING A NEW CLASS

To attract the finest students available, the Georgetown Law Center engaged KINETIK, Inc., to create a guide to the center for prospective students. This "yield piece" differs from a traditional viewbook. Georgetown's viewbook goes to anyone inquiring about the school, whereas the yeild piece goes only to accepted students. This collateral is meant to inspire accepted prospects to become Georgetown students. Georgetown is one of the nation's top law schools, but recruiting the best talent takes a well-thought-out approach in this competitive market. To succeed, the guide needed to convey the rich tradition of excellence at Georgetown while generating excitement in prospects about the school and living in the Washington, D.C., region.

The guide helps prospects begin bonding with their new home.

Direct Access

KINETIK began its research by examining materials from competing law schools. Though that provided a comparative starting point, KINETIK also made good use of its direct access to its target audience for research purposes. Prospective law students participate in a very active online community, so after the students have selected a law school, Georgetown sends a survey to those who chose a different university. KINETIK took the opportunity to include questions relating to the design and content of other universities' welcome packets, which helped inform the next iteration of the Georgetown material. KINETIK's questions focused on how the welcome materials influenced students' decisions on which school to attend. (Many students had received multiple acceptance letters from various law programs.)

Georgetown also provided KINETIK access to a group of first year students known as "student ambassadors." This access provided a good measuring stick for the success of the acceptance materials. The designers met with this group to find out priorities for prospective Georgetown Law students. KINETIK focused on what influenced their decision to attend Georgetown, what they were surprised to find out when they started in the program, and what could be emphasized in future yield pieces. Because the KINETIK yield piece has multiple components, this summative survey helped the designers learn which specific components were useful and which were not.

Unusual Approach, Outstanding Results

The results of the research led the designers to a unique approach. They created a box of materials welcoming prospects not only to Georgetown but also to Washington, D.C. The solution is much more substantial and personal than a traditional welcome kit. The concept follows a day in the life of real Georgetown Law students, and provides details about the school that any prospective student might want to know, such as the diversity of Georgetown students or the flavor of the different neighborhoods around the school. Beyond that, the guide helps prospects begin bonding with their new home by including copies of local publications, apartment guides, insider information, and other special details that build a connection with the school and region. Photos, design, and copy all support the needs highlighted by the research: accessibility and generating interest.

The unconventional approach was bold, and the large box was unusual—which created both better visibility and better recall. Potential students emailed one another to find out if they too had gotten a "box from Georgetown." In the end, research enabled KINETIK to identify not only information that the client wanted to convey, but also information that the target audience wished to receive.[29]

Opposite
Sketches and color studies allowed KINETIK to explore the formal presentation of the marketing collateral, as well as to troubleshoot structural issues of packaging, and determine the usability of the contents.

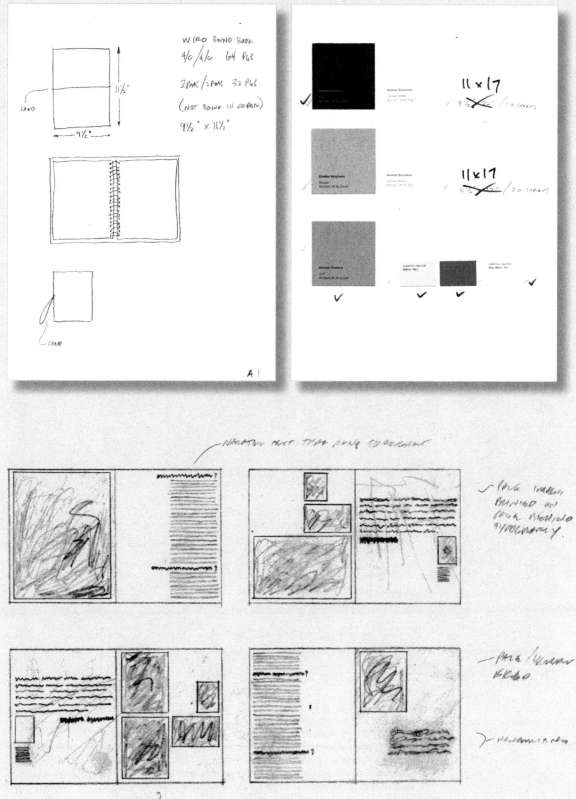

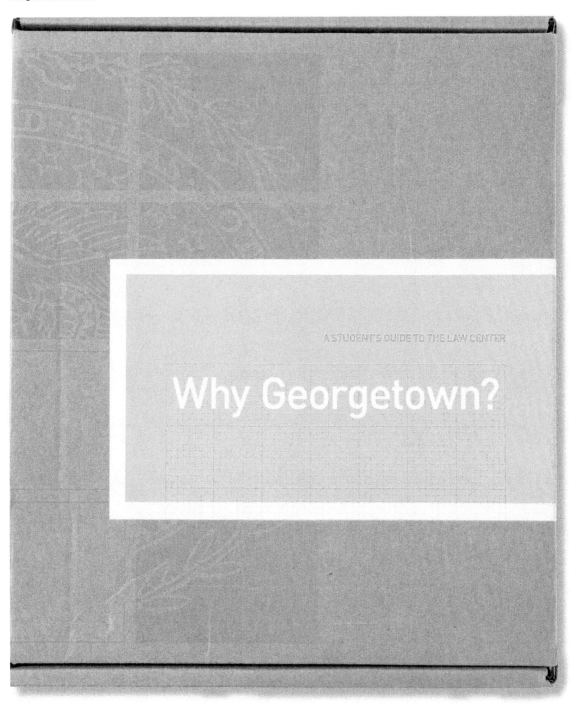

A STUDENT'S GUIDE TO THE LAW CENTER

Why Georgetown?

Above
Interviewing first-year's about their application and acceptance experience, KINETIK was able to develop unique collateral that would stand out in the minds of students, while providing prospects a glimpse of life at Georgetown Law. With students calling and emailing one another to see if their friends had also received a "box from Georgetown," the package created the buzz the firm and the university had hoped for.

This Page
KINETIK went beyond the traditional contents of an acceptance packet, providing Georgetown student prospects with lifestyle information that would make the transition to their new home easy to imagine. Students received information on neighborhoods, cultural centers, utilities, maps of key areas, and even postcards to send home.

This Page
KINETIK was able to engage Georgetown students by creating a welcome kit that was user-centered. This insert provides students with ample information about the Georgetown experience, showcasing local *landmarks, neighborhoods, and activities. An energetic color palette matches the excitement of a new school, a new career, and new life experiences.*

PROJECT:	CLIENT:	INTENDED AUDIENCE:	CREDITS:
Harmony, a magazine for senior citizens	*Harmony* magazine for DHA Memorial Trust, Mumbai, India	urban, educated, middle-class; Age group of above 55 years	Ashwini Deshpande and Sudhir Sharma, both founder-directors and principal designers of Elephant Strategy + Design

↓

RESEARCHING FROM SCRATCH

When designing India's first magazine for senior citizens, Elephant Strategy + Design faced several developmental and aesthetic issues. First and foremost, very little data that applied readily to magazine design existed for their target demographic. Further research of the target group showed that senior citizens most often read newspapers. This helped define some editorial content decisions.

Because the client recognized a marketing opportunity, focusing on the unique needs of Indian senior citizens, the design team chose to focus primarily on those needs in their research efforts—and ultimately in their designs. Elephant began by analyzing various magazines dedicated to senior citizen lifestyles from around the world. This literature review helped determine basic structural rules, such as picture ratio and font size.

At no point did we want to create something that would remind the readers of their age.

Surveys Provide a Breakthrough

Because they were creating a new publication, Elephant wanted to target the intended audience with surveys. Not much data was available on the preferences or choices of Indian seniors, so Elephant sought them out at senior citizens' clubs, walking parks, common recreational areas within housing complexes, temples, and restaurants.

The surveys sought an understanding of the physical limitations and necessities that would influence the viewer's reading experience. They asked questions about reading style and habits, as well as the requirements and preferences seniors placed on their publications. Questions about preferred topics, authors, and journalists were included. Subjects were even asked about stylistic preferences.

The next phase involved beta testing the complete project through focus groups. When most design decisions were applied and Elephant needed to reconfirm certain assumptions and analyses before going live, they invited journalists, celebrities, and graphic designers—all above 55 years of age—for feedback on design and style of the magazine.

A Successful Launch

Elephant says that certain aesthetic and structural decisions regarding fonts, grids, and color choices would have bypassed the target group completely if attention had not been paid to user-centered research. This information was especially critical because Elephant had no opinions or assumptions about the project, having never before created a project specifically for an older audience.

"Every magazine designer dreams of making a very sleek, stylish and edgy product," says Ashwini Deshpande of Elephant. "We refrained ourselves from doing anything for the sake of aesthetics. Our simple brief to ourselves was to create an 'easy, comfortable, and interesting' magazine for the audience." None of these values was to be traded for stylish aesthetics.

"Just like children's books have a different sense of aesthetics, primarily due to heavy picture content and large fonts, we defined a fine-tuned aesthetics for the older people. The challenge was to get it right without having to explicitly pronounce it. At no point did we want to create something that would remind the readers of their age."

The result of the efforts was a set of design and content rules that helped provide a user-friendly magazine, delivering information to this unique target audience in an appealing and invigorating fashion.

Top
Elephant's research team catches
their target market out and about.

Above
The Harmony identity was
designed as a symbol and a
masthead. Emphasis was placed
on the legibility and clarity.

Harmony Magazine
Maker Chamber IV, 4th Floor, 222, Narimal Point, Mumbai - 400 021
Tel : +91 22 30325000, 22842929. Fax : +91 22 22852217

Above
Promotional items were
developed to increase
awareness for India's first
magazine targeted specifically
at a senior citizen audience.

Opposite
Elephant launched a multistage
research process for their
design of Harmony, India's first
magazine for senior citizens.

Recognizing a lack of information
about the target audience, the
design team gathered surveys
and interviews to inform design
choices. Careful consideration

was paid to the physical needs of
seniors, with special consideration
given to type choices and image-
to-content ratios.

PROJECT:
Activmobs: increasing activity in older people

CLIENT:
public benefit

INTENDED AUDIENCE:
overweight community members

CREDITS:
Design Council RED Unit with Kent County Council and the residents of Park Wood

A GROWING PROBLEM

Poor diets and sedentary lifestyles are contributing to a healthcare crisis in the United Kingdom. Recognizing the need for change, the Design Council's RED Unit began several projects to encourage preventative action by the general public. RED created Activmobs to fight obesity and its health risks by encouraging physical activity in citizens of Kent County.

People Drive the Solution

RED chose to focus on individuals for their research and consequential design decisions. Rather than replicate health club appeals, the council developed the idea of Activmobs, a community-building service that offers support systems and organizational tools instead of workout regimens. Initial interviews and focus groups defined this strategy, and the designers worked with local stakeholders—most notably the residents of Park Wood, whose feedback proved invaluable.

The designers worked with local stakeholders, whose feedback proved invaluable.

To tackle the project, the RED team brought together a diverse group of consultants, from product designers to branding specialists. The team also received research input from various experts, including policy analysts, health-care professionals, personal trainers, psychologists, and others.

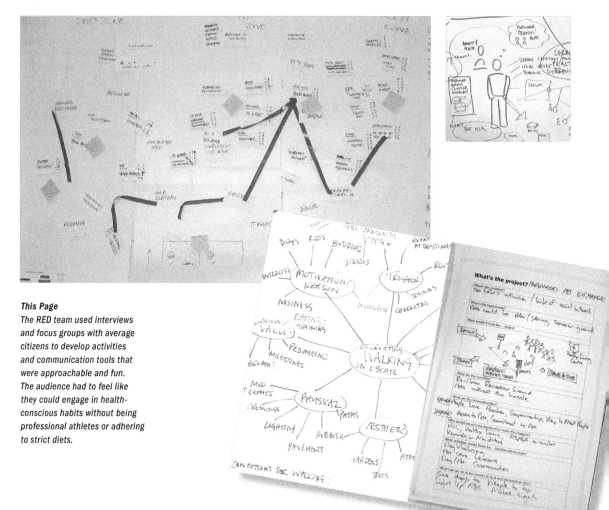

This Page

The RED team used interviews and focus groups with average citizens to develop activities and communication tools that were approachable and fun. The audience had to feel like they could engage in health-conscious habits without being professional athletes or adhering to strict diets.

Initial Research

The project began with two days of intensive research, including a workshop with local stakeholders. The team spent a day at Park Wood to get a feel for the area and to examine the background demographic and health data. During this time, they found residents willing to get involved with the project. Visiting six volunteer participants in their homes, they conducted interviews to determine day-to-day routines and interests. The RED team designed a set of flashcards, each depicting a different activity, from walking to swimming to going to the pub. Participants chose three categories: those they do, those they would like to do, and those they would never do. Researchers also conducted an "activity audit" in respondents' homes to better determine how much physical activity was part of the daily routine of each interviewee. Finally, at the end of the session, the researchers spent an hour with participants, focused on understanding the experience of a single "activity," such as walking to local shops or taking the dog out.

From these sessions, the team created brief sketches of the lives of the participants, providing an overview of their hobbies, lifestyles, and exercise regimes. To get a full range of profiles of the people of Park Wood, the team held a series of workshops with community leaders and social workers to fill in any portraits that might be missing.

Overcoming Obstacles

Research showed that being healthy and living an active life is difficult for the people of Park Wood. It seemed difficult for individuals to prioritize activity over other commitments. Although the target audience understood that exercise was good for them, the residents clearly needed motivation and help removing barriers and releasing untapped resources.

The design team therefore sought to build a system to encourage activity that addressed the micro-motivations of individuals and overcame widespread objections to activity for activity's sake. The solution capitalized on individuals' passions and interests by harnessing them as a resource to motivate others. Acitvmobs removed barriers to activity by inspiring individuals to form teams based on shared interests. "Mobs" form voluntarily, and different people get motivated for different reasons, such as:

· *Achieving the physical benefits of activity (fitness, weight loss, good health)*

· *Socializing and having fun through shared interests*

· *Being inspired by fellow "mob" members*

The Designer's Role

Because Activmobs' success is based on participant interaction and influence, the design solution would have to raise awareness of the program and provide incentives and tools to make network building easy and fun. Communication pieces needed to foster a sense of ownership, because each Activmob is created

Opposite
To take some of the burden off of the social health-care system, the Design Council RED unit assembled a multidisciplinary team of researchers and designers to tackle engaging the British public in healthier lifestyles. RED created Activmobs to fight obesity and sedentary habits by encouraging citizens to take on approachable physical activities.

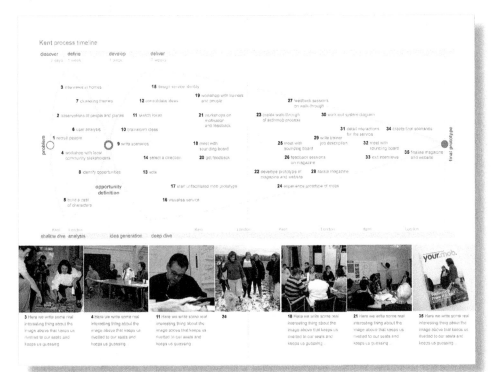

Kent process timeline

discover   define   develop   deliver

activ.mob.

wearemobs.org

www.wearemobs.org

wearemobs.org

and administered by the very individuals it aims to help. The following design collateral was developed in support of this mission:

· *A prototype magazine clearly explains Activmobs and gives access to the resources necessary to form or join a group.*

· *Activmob Logs and Wellbeing Cards make tracking progress easy.*

· *Vouchers for local services and businesses provide incentives for mobs to achieve fitness goals.*

An accessible, friendly website ties all the elements together and provides online access to all necessary resources.

The results of this charter program have been very encouraging. More and more residents are getting fit with the help of Activmobs, and there are plans to expand the program throughout the U.K. The project charts another victory for RED and the Design Council and provides a powerful example of the value of design research, strategy, and action.[30]

Opposite: Top
An Activmob, out for a group walk.

Bottom
A magazine was created to spotlight different Activmobs and the activities in which they were engaged. The publication also provides information about membership, activities, healthier eating habits, and how to find Activmob personal trainers. Images of real Activmob members, instead of models, dominate the document.

Exercise is good for you

Everyone knows exercise is good for you, but it's not easy to be active. You have to motivate yourself to get started and keep going, as well as finding the time and the money.

The activmob platform supports small self-organised groups doing regular activity in a way that fits with their lifestyle, interests and abilities. It helps people to get active and stay active.

The aim of this project was to increase activity in people aged 40-70 and to reduce the likelihood of obesity and age related illness such as fractures, osteoporosis, alzheimers and diabetes. The project is part of the RED unit's health project and was co-designed with the residents of Park Wood, Kent, in partnership with Kent County Council. It will be launched in June 2005.

RED is a new unit at the Design Council challenging accepted thinking on economic and social problems through design innovation. We run rapid live projects in order to develop new thinking and practical design solutions in the form of systems, services and products. Our team is inter-disciplinary and our approach human centred.

See www.designcouncil.org.uk/RED for further details. Email Judec@designcouncil.org.uk

Find out more
your.mob
- The protoype magazine

wearemobs.org
- The protoype website

tell me more...
- Activmobs introduction
- How to join a mob
- Starting a mob
- Activmob trainers
- The vouchers
- Setting your goals

This site requires QuickTime and Flash. They can be obtained here:
QuickTime, Flash

Left
The Activmob website provides members with a series of online tools that can help them build their Activmob community, motivate each other, or track individual progress toward a healthier lifestyle.

NOTES

↓

1 László Moholy-Nagy, *The New Vision: Fundamentals of Bauhaus Design, Painting, Sculpture, and Architecture*, (New York: W.W. Norton & Company, 1938).

2 Henry Dreyfuss, *Designing for People* (New York: Allworth Press, 2003).

3 For more on the ACNielsen company, go to www.acnielsen.com/site/index.shtml

4 To view the American Anthropological Association's statement on professional ethics, go to www.aaanet.org/committees/ethics/ethcode.htm

5 Alan Cooper, *The Inmates Are Running the Asylum: Why High-Tech Products Drive Us Crazy and How to Restore the Sanity* (Indianapolis: Sams Publishing, 1999).

6 For more about cultural associations with color, read *Color Design Workbook*. Adams Morioka and Terry Stone, *Color Design Workbook: A Real-World Guide to Using Color in Graphic Design* (Gloucester, MA: Rockport Publishers, 2006).

7 For more on Pantone, Inc., go to www.pantone.com

8 For more on the Color Association of the United States, go to www.colorassociation.com

9 For more on the Color Marketing Group, go to www.colormarketing.org

10 David Williams, "Color Perception Is Not in the Eye of the Beholder: It's in the Brain," news release, University of Rochester, October 25, 2005. Available online at www.rochester.edu/news/show.php?id=2299

11 For more about information literacy goals on an international scale, visit the United Nations Educational Scientific and Cultural Organization (UNESCO) web portal at portal.unesco.org/education/en/ev.php-URL_ID=40338&URL_DO=DO_TOPIC&URL_SECTION=201.html

12 For more about the Big6™, go to www.big6.com

13 For more details about AIGA's Design Framework, go to www.aiga.org/content.cfm?ContentID=2124

14 To view case studies that use AIGA's Designing Framework, go to designing.aiga.org

15 For in-depth documentation of the Design Council's process, go to www.design-council.org.uk

16 For TeacherVision's printable graphic organizers, go to www.teachervision.fen.com/graphic-organizers/printable/6293.html

17 For information on ConceptDraw's Mindmap, go to www.conceptdraw.com/en/products/mindmap/main.php

18 For information on ThinkMap's Visual Thesaurus, go to www.visualthesaurus.com/

19 For detailed information on the Design Council's Design Index, or to download a PDF of the Design Index Report 2005, go to www.designcouncil.org.uk

20 For more about the Big6™, go to www.big6.com

21 For more about the process described in this Expert Voice, read Paul Nini "Sharpening one's axe: making a case for a comprehensive approach to research in the graphic design process," (paper presentation, AIGA Future History 2004 Design Education Conference, Chicago). Available online at http://futurehistory.aiga.org/content.cfm?Alias=fh_speakerssub2

22 To try out the Web Color Visualizer, go to www.ideo.com/visualizer.html

23 To try out Color Schemer, go to www.colorschemer.com/online.html

24 *Election Design: Models for Improvement*, "Ballot Design Basics," AIGA Design for Democracy, 2002. Available at www.designfordemocracy.org/resources/content/2/3/8/5/documents/ballotdesignbasics.pdf

25 Radio interview conducted with the president of the Voting Experience Redesign Intiative project, BBC London, January 11, 2001. www.designfordemocracy.org/content.cfm?Alias=designfordemocracynews

26 SEGD Members can access SEGDTalk forum for free. For more information, go to www.segd.org

27 A great resource for typographic family descriptions is www.thinkingwithtype.com by Ellen Lupton, a companion to the book of the same name. Ellen Lupton, *Thinking with Type: A Critical Guide for Designers, Writers, Editors, and Students* (New York: Princeton Architectural Press, 2004).

28 To view a Design Council case study on the Vitacress redesign, go to www.designcouncil.org.uk

29 To view an AIGA Designing Framework case study on the Georgetown Law Center Guide, go to designing.aiga.org/content.cfm/georgetownlawcentergeorgetownlawcenter

30 For detailed information on the Activmobs project, or other RED health projects, go to www.designcouncil.org.uk/mt/red/health/index.html

GLOSSARY
OF
TERMS

Benchmark Testing The act of making comparisons to a pre-established standard against which other iterations are evaluated.

Color Psychology The study of the affect colors have on human behavior.

Competitor Analysis The process of evaluating the strengths and weaknesses of an organization's competitors.

Competitor Profiling The establishment of personas for corporations, which helps to identify motivations, goals, and possibly the actions of an organization's competitors.

Demographics Collections of statistical data that describe a group of people. Common demographic variables include race, age, gender, and income.

Ethnographic Research A research technique used by anthropologists to understand the link between human behavior and culture.

Focus Groups A social science tool in which organized discussions, led by a moderator, are held in order to collect market research.

Formative Research Research conducted at the beginning of a project to help define the problem to be solved.

Graphic Organizers Visual tools that help designers connect concepts and see the relationships between information sets.

Information Literacy A learning strategy that emphasizes the ability to recognize when information is needed, and to hone the skills to find, evaluate, analyze, and effectively use that information.

Iterative Design A design process that uses a series of prototyping, testing, and refining cycles to reach a solution.

Literature Review A comprehensive investigation of all documents, publications, articles, and books available within a specific area of study.

Marketing Research A form of sociology that focuses on the understanding of human behavior as it applies to a market-based economy, often specific to consumer preferences.

Market Segment A subgroup or classification of a larger market; market segments may be delineated by any number of qualitative or quantitative criteria.

Media Scanning A process of scrutinizing a competitor's publicly available corporate communications (such as annual reports and press releases), ad placement, messaging, and discernible brand presence, often across multiple media channels.

Observational Research The systematic process of viewing and recording human behavior and cultural phenomena without questioning, communicating, or interacting with the group being studied.

Personas Fabricated models of end users that are created to identify motivations, expectations, and goals.

Photo Ethnography A field exercise in which subjects are asked to record their daily experiences with still or video cameras. Individual cases can be combined in order to develop a broader understanding of a community under study.

Primary Research Research conducted specifically for an individual problem or project.

Proprietary A unique service or offering that is exclusive property of the owner or inventor.

Psychographics A quantitative tactic used to measure the subjective beliefs of the group being studied. Common psychographic variables might include religious beliefs, music tastes, and personality traits.

Public Domain Publications, products, processes, and information not protected under patent or copyright that belong to the community at large.

Qualitative Research A research approach that measures subjective data such as words, images, and opinions.

Quantitative Research A research approach that measures objective data such as variables, quantities, and measurements, and analyzes the relationships between collected information sets.

Questionnaires A tactic for collecting quantitative information by asking participants a set of questions in specific order. Participants in a questionnaire answer questions by filling out a piece of paper or online; questions are not administered orally (see survey).

ROI (Return on Investment) The measure of a performance by comparing the cost of an investment to the results that it produced.

Secondary Research Reviewing a collection of data or findings that have previously been published by an outside party, for an alternative function.

Summative Research Used to frame and decipher the outcome of an investigative process. It confirms that the original hypothesis is correct or illustrates that it is flawed.

Surveys A tactic for collecting quantitative information by asking participants a set of questions in specific order. When a researcher administers the questions it is called a survey or structured interview.

Target Audience/Market The group or segment to which a communication is being directed.

Triangulation Using three or more different research techniques to find areas of overlap. Common results, called convergence, are considered to be the most reliable.

User Testing A broad range of techniques designed to measure a product's ability to satisfy the needs of the end user, such as accessibility, functionality, and ease of use, while also meeting project requirements, such as budget, size, and technical requirements.

Visual Anthropology A field research tactic that uses visual media to aid interpretations of cultural behavior. Visual anthropology differs from photo ethnography by placing the camera in the trained hands of the researcher, rather than in the untrained hands of a subject.

Visual Exploration A method of primary research most commonly used by designers for solving problems of form and communication (studies might include variations of color, imagery, typography, and structure).

Visualization A rapid prototyping tool used to make concepts understood.

Web Analytics A form of quantitative analysis that uses concrete metrics to track user behavior online.

INDEX

CONTRIBUTORS

CASE STUDIES

Baseman Design Associates
221 Mather Road
Jenkintown, PA 19046
USA
215.885.7157
www.basemandesign.com

dara creative*
19 Magennis Place
Dublin 2, Ireland
353.(0)1.672.5222
www.daracreative.ie

Elephant Strategy + Design
13 Kumar Srushti,
Nda-Pashan Road
Bavdhan, Pune 411 021
India
+91.20.22951055/9
www.elephantdesign.com

Financial Designs
No. 2, 52 St. James Road
Sutton, Surrey, SM1 2TS
United Kingdom
+44.20.8404.2337
www.findes.com

***HOW* Magazine, F&W Publications**
4700 East Galbraith Road
Cincinnati, OH 45236
USA
513.531.2690
www.howdesign.com

Landesberg Design
USA
412.381.2220
www.landesbergdesign.com

KINETIK
1436 U Street NW,
Suite 404
Washington, DC 20009
USA
202.797.0605
www.kinetikcom.com

Meyer & Liechty, Inc.
919 West 500
North Lindon, UT 84042
USA
801.785.1155
www.ml-studio.com

Pentagram Design
1508 West Fifth Street
Austin, TX 78703
USA
512.476.3076
www.pentagram.co.uk

RED, Design Council
34 Bow Street
London WC2E 7DL
United Kingdom
+44.20.7420.5200
www.designcouncil.org.uk/mt/red/

Rule29
303 West State Street
Geneva, IL 60134
USA
630.262.1009
www.rule29.com

Schwartz Powell Design
320 West 48th Street
Minneapolis, MN 55419
USA
612.874.6700
www.schwartzpowell.com

Sterling Brands
350 Fifth Avenue
New York, NY 10118
USA
212.329.4600
www.sterlingbrands.com

Studio Blue
800 West Huron
Suite 3N
Chicago, IL 60622
USA
312.243.2241
www.studioblueinc.com

Studio/Lab
1 East Wacker Drive,
Suite 3030
Chicago, IL 60601
USA
312.873.7700
www.studiolab.com

CREDITS

Portrait of Arthur C. Nielsen Sr. courtesy of **ACNeilsen**

Designing Framework courtesy of **AIGA**

Big6™ information literacy model courtesy of **Big6 Associates, LLC**

Genz-Ryan Rebranding courtesy of **Catalyst Studios**

Postcards and photos courtesy of the **Cleveland Memory Project** at Cleveland State University, special thanks to **Dr. Walter Leedy**

Screen shots of color-matching software courtesy of **ColorSchemer**

The Design Process, Case Studies website screen shot, and Design Index graphs courtesy of **Design Council**

Website screen shot courtesy of **Design Management Institute**

Media Kit courtesy of *Dwell* **Magazine**

Nexterna Marketing Campaign courtesy of **Eleven19 Communications, Inc.**

A Designer's Research Manual sketches, Douglas Goldsmith website screen shots, and Nance College viewbook materials courtesy of **Enspace, A Creative Think Tank**

Joe + Josephine diagram courtesy of **Henry Dreyfuss Associates**

Visual anthropology lab photos courtesy of **Dr. Barbara Hoffman**, Cleveland State University

Patient Journey Framework diagram courtesy of **IDEO**

Assorted stock photography, **Istock Photo**

Restaurant Kolumbia visualization materials courtesy of **KINETIK**, special thanks to **Sam Shelton**

Student annual report courtesy of **Jared Lavey**

Photos of the Leede usability lab courtesy of **The Leede Research Group**

Website screen shot courtesy of **Logoworks**

The work of **László Moholy-Nagy** courtesy of his daughter, **Hattula Moholy-Nagy**

Survey research tool courtesy of **OpinionLab**

Color forecasts courtesy of **Pantone, Inc.**

Web analytics screen shot courtesy of **Point In Space**

Student sketches and AIGA recruiting posters courtesy of **Gary Rozanc**

Website screen shot courtesy of **StockLayouts LLC**

Visual Thesaurus screen shot courtesy of **Thinkmap**

EXPERT VOICES

Michael Bond
Bond Coyne and Associates
United Kingdom
www.bondandcoyne.co.uk

Ashwini Deshpande
Elephant Strategy + Design
13 Kumar Srushti,
Nda-Pashan Road
Bavdhan, Pune 411 021
India
+91.20.22951055/9
www.elephantdesign.com

Paul Nini
Ohio State University
373 Hopkins Hall,
128 N Oval Mall
Columbus, OH 43201
USA
614.292.1077
design.osu.edu

Dan Overfield
Villanova University
800 Lancaster Avenue
Villanova, PA 19085
USA
610.519.8129
www.villanova.edu

DJ Stout
Pentagram Design
1508 West Fifth Street
Austin, TX 78703
USA
512.476.3076
www.pentagram.co.uk

Elizabeth Tunstall
Design for Democracy + University of Illinois at Chicago
820 West Jackson Boulevard,
Suite 330
Chicago, IL 60607
USA
312.996.9768
designfordemocracy.aiga.org
www.uic.edu

BIBLIOGRAPHY

Bestly, Russell, and Ian Noble. *Visual Research: An Introduction to Research Methodologies in Graphic Design*. New York: AVA Publishing, 2005.

Colin, Kim and IDEO. *Extra Spatial*. San Francisco: Chronicle Books, 2003.

Cooper, Alan. *The Inmates Are Running the Asylum: Why High Tech Products Drive Us Crazy and How to Restore the Sanity*. Indianapolis: Sams Publishing, 1999.

Dreyfuss, Henry. *Designing for People*. New York: Allworth Press, 2003. First published 1955 by Simon and Schuster.

Laurel, Brenda, ed. *Design Research: Methods and Perspectives*. Cambridge, Massachusetts: MIT Press, 2003.

Moholy-Nagy, László. *The New Vision: Fundamentals of Bauhaus Design, Painting, Sculpture, and Architecture*. New York: W.W. Norton & Company, 1938.

Stone, Terry, and Adams Morioka. *Color Design Workbook: A Real-World Guide to Using Color in Graphic Design*. Gloucester, Massachusetts: Rockport Publishers, 2006.

ABOUT THE AUTHORS

AUTHORS' ACKNOWLEDGEMENTS

JENN + KEN VISOCKY O'GRADY

Jenn + Ken Visocky O'Grady are partners in business and life. The couple cofounded Enspace, a creative think tank where designers, writers, marketers, and even the occasional historian collaborate to enhance communication. The firm's work has been recognized by numerous organizations and featured in magazines and books. Aspiring design evangelists, Jenn + Ken have traveled the country jurying competitions and presenting workshops and lectures. They also spin daily chalk talks on the value of design in the classroom, though there they practice solo—Jenn is an Associate Professor at Cleveland State University, Ken an Assistant Professor at Kent State University.

Born-and-raised Clevelanders, the couple is proud to claim Ohio as their home.

This is their first book.

THANK YOU!

This book is a collaborative effort, and would not have been possible without the shared experiences and candor of our contributors. We are inspired by their work and honored by their participation.

The colleagues and friends we have met through AIGA professional circles have been invaluable resources. Special thanks to Christopher Liechty and Christopher Vice for sharing their wisdom and ample connections!

Enspace would be seriously limping if our colleagues, Paul Perchinske, Craig Ihms, and Amir Khosravi weren't there to pull our slack while we worked on this book project. We're indebted for the endless design critiques, last minute proofing, and steady pep talks. Craig's experience as a professional journalist was essential in shaping the case study section of the book.

Tom Humphrey, Kristin Ellison, and Regina Grenier have been mentors and guides as we navigate the world of publishing, and Rebecca Ranallo-Kahl provided expert research assistance.

We are indebted to the professors who inspired us, and to the students who keep us on our toes.

Our parents raised us on bedtime stories, piles of books, assorted art supplies, and a steady stream of expectation and encouragement. They were our first and remain our most influential role models of professional passion and work ethic. How do you thank someone for a lifetime of opportunity? We hope "we love you" will suffice.

Our friends and family have put up with belated celebrations, cancelled dates, and long quiet spells with no contact while we worked in a cave on this book. Hopefully they'll still take our calls now that it's complete.

To the next phase...

CPSIA information can be obtained at www.ICGtesting.com
Printed in the USA
LVOW05s1930250915

455743LV00031B/128/P